CLAUDE KING
with Meditations by ANDREW MURRAY

Come to the Lord's Table

A 28-DAY DEVOTIONAL GUIDE

LifeWay Press®
Nashville, Tennessee

P9-BYK-314

Published by LifeWay Press® • © 2006 Claude V. King • Reprinted 2018

No part of this book may be reproduced or transmitted in any form or by any means, electronic or mechanical, including photocopying and recording, or by any information storage or retrieval system, except as may be expressly permitted in writing by the publisher. Requests for permission should be addressed in writing to LifeWay Press®; One LifeWay Plaza; Nashville, TN 37234.

ISBN 978-1-4158-3203-5 • Item 001315091

Dewey decimal classification: 264.36
Subject headings: LORD'S SUPPER \ JESUS CHRIST—CRUCIFIXION

In 1897 Andrew Murray published *The Lord's Table: A Help to the Right Observance of the Holy Supper.* Meditations from *The Lord's Table* have been updated and edited by Claude King. They will be identified by indented and colored text and the reference (LT, p. #). A complete public-domain text of *The Lord's Table* by Murray is available on the Internet at ccel.org/m/murray/lords_table/.

The Scriptures used in Andrew Murray's meditations are revised from the public-domain text of *The Lord's Table*, which was originally written in Dutch and later translated into English. When referenced in this book, they are marked (AM).

Unless otherwise noted, all Scripture quotations are taken from the Holman Christian Standard Bible®, copyright © 1999, 2000, 2001, 2002, 2003, 2009 by Holman Bible Publishers. Used by permission. Scripture quotations marked NIV are taken from the Holy Bible, NEW INTERNATIONAL VERSION®. Copyright © 1973, 1978, 1984 by Biblica Inc. All rights reserved worldwide. Used by permission. Scripture quotations marked KJV are taken from the King James Version of the Bible.

Underlining and italics in Scripture quotations in this book are used to emphasize words or phrases and are not part of the original Scripture texts or translations.

To order additional copies of this resource, write to LifeWay Resources Customer Service; One LifeWay Plaza; Nashville, TN 37234; fax 615-251-5933; phone toll free 800-458-2772; email orderentry@lifeway.com; order online at LifeWay.com; or visit the LifeWay Christian Store serving you.

Printed in the United States of America

Groups Ministry Publishing • LifeWay Resources • One LifeWay Plaza • Nashville, TN 37234

Contents

Preface

In 1989 Richard Owen Roberts of Wheaton, Illinois, introduced me and other leaders in my denomination to the biblical pattern for corporate repentance—the solemn assembly (sacred assembly, NIV). We began to study sacred assemblies in Scripture to understand their connections to revival. Sacred assemblies were occasions for God's people collectively to worship Him, to repent of personal and corporate sin, to remember His special blessings on them, and to anticipate future blessings. The prescribed sacred assemblies (or holy convocations) for Israel included the Sabbath (see Lev. 23:3) and seven other days of sacred assembly: the first (Passover) and seventh days of the Feast of Unleavened Bread (see Lev. 23:4-8), the Feast of Weeks (Pentecost, see Lev. 23:15-21), the Feast of Trumpets (see Lev. 23:23-25), the Day of Atonement (see Lev. 23:26-32), and the first and eighth days of the Feast of Tabernacles (see Lev. 23:33-36).

Sacred assemblies were times for God's people to confess and repent of their sins. They were times to renew the covenant relationship with the Lord and return to Him in faithful love and obedience. They were times for worship and sacrifice, feasting and fasting. Even with these regular opportunities to renew fellowship with God, His people tended to depart from Him and from obedience to His commands. Spiritual leaders knew the sacred assembly was a time for corporate repentance in the face of God's righteous judgments (see Joel 1–2). <u>A number of national revivals in the Old Testament occurred in response to sacred assemblies.</u>

The term *sacred assembly* is not used in the New Testament. However, Jesus and His disciples celebrated the last supper on one of God's prescribed sacred assemblies—the Feast of Passover. The first disciples were celebrating a sacred assembly when the Holy Spirit was poured out at Pentecost. The church of our day also needs regular opportunities for individuals and the church to renew their relationships with the Lord—to remember and renew the new-covenant relationship they have with Him. I believe the Lord's Supper (or Communion or Eucharist) is probably our best and most natural opportunity to celebrate a sacred assembly of God's people. Properly observed, it can be a time of genuine revival among God's people. It can be a time to turn the hearts of God's people back to our Lord who died for us—the One who is to be our first love.

Many people are deeply concerned over the casual way modern Christians participate in the Lord's table. The Apostle Paul sent a warning to the Corinthian church. It should cause us to be concerned: "Whoever eats

4

the bread or drinks the cup of the Lord in an unworthy way will be guilty of sin against the body and blood of the Lord. So a man should examine himself; in this way he should eat of the bread and drink of the cup. For whoever eats and drinks without recognizing the body, eats and drinks judgment on himself. This is why many are sick and ill among you, and many have fallen asleep" (1 Cor. 11:27-30).

Have you ever gone to the Lord's table to partake of the bread and juice (or wine) and left the service unmoved and unchanged? I have. When I partake of the supper in a casual way, I unintentionally say, "Lord, Your death on the cross wasn't that important." How grieved God must be when I care so little for the great sacrifice He made for my salvation.

Churches in the past took the Lord's Supper very seriously. Many churches would take a day, a weekend, or even a week or more for special services to help God's people prepare themselves to partake of the Lord's table in a worthy manner. These days were sometimes called pre-Communion days. Some groups would even fence the Lord's table to prevent unworthy participants from defiling the event. Only those who had adequately prepared themselves were permitted to partake.

I was explaining this to a missionary from west Africa when he exclaimed, "That's what happened to me in Africa!" He went on to explain that he went to pastor a church during his first term as a missionary. One Sunday he realized that the congregation had not celebrated the Lord's Supper since his arrival. He announced in the morning service that they would celebrate the supper that evening.

An elder on the front row began to weep and said, "Pastor, you must not ask us to do this. We always spend at least a day preparing ourselves for the Lord's Supper. We haven't had time to prepare. It would be offensive to God for us to come unprepared." The missionary realized they treated the Lord's Supper with much greater respect than he was accustomed to. Believers need to return to celebrating the Lord's Supper in a worthy manner.

In 1897 the famed author and pastor Andrew Murray of South Africa wrote a book for his congregation to help them observe the holy supper in a worthy manner. Members spent a week prior to the supper in personal preparation, using Murray's book *The Lord's Table* as their devotional guide. The book also provided prayers and meditations for the day of the celebration. Then members spent the week following the celebration reflecting on changes that should take place in their lives because of Christ's sacrifice for them.

When I first read *The Lord's Table*, I realized we needed a similar work for churches today. From time to time I'll include meditations from Murray's book to stir your love and response to the Lord. In his preface Murray wrote:

One chief cause why some do not grow more in grace is that they do not take time to <u>converse with the Lord in secret</u>. Spiritual, divine truth does not become my possession all at once. Although I understand what I read, although I consent heartily to it, although I receive it, it may speedily fade away and be forgotten. I must give it time to become fixed and rooted in me, to become united and identified with me by private meditation. Christians … <u>give your Lord time to transfer His heavenly thoughts to your inner life. When you have read a portion, set yourselves in silence before God. Take time to remain before Him until He has made His word living and</u> powerful in your souls. Then it will become the life and the power of your life (LT, pp. 7–8).

This book is designed to help you do just what Murray suggested. I've prepared this book to help us celebrate the Lord's table in a way that will honor the Lord. I never again want to go to the Lord's table without sensing a nearness and communion with my Savior. I want to participate in a worthy manner that will draw me near to Him and bring Him pleasure in my worship.

My prayer is that the Lord will use this simple tool to renew your church as you give special attention to remembering the Lord's death until He comes again. Take time each day to use this guide to help you prepare your mind, heart, and life for your meeting at the Lord's table. If we properly examine ourselves and participate in a worthy manner, the Lord's table can be a time to renew the new covenant with our Lord. It will be a time to return to our first love. It will be a time to repent of sin that has crept into our lives and relationships. Every observance will be another invitation to reconcile any broken relationships in the body of Christ. The result will be a clean and pure church that loves and faithfully obeys her Lord until the day we sit down as a pure bride at the marriage supper of the Lamb. Such a clean church will be far more fruitful in obeying the Lord's final command to expand His kingdom by making disciples of the nations.

Use this book as your guide for personal preparation. Use it as a guide for personal cleansing. Focus your attention on the wounded Savior and the high price He paid for your forgiveness. Rekindle your memories of His blessed life and return to your first love for Him. May you present your life as a worthy and living sacrifice to Him. May He fill you with a new sense of wonder at His love for you. I pray that this book will help your church join in sacred assembly and prepare the bride of Christ for her marriage to the Lamb.

Day 1 ~ God So Loved He Gave His Son

Oct 29

> *"God loved the world in this way:*
> *He gave His One and Only Son,*
> *so that everyone who believes in Him*
> *will not perish but have eternal life."*
>
> John 3:16

What good news that is for you and me! God loved us so much that He gave the life of His Son, Jesus Christ, so that we could know life at its best for all eternity. Of all people on earth, Christians are most blessed. I don't know about you, but I'm overwhelmed to think the Creator of the universe <u>has such an interest in me.</u>

Unfortunately, life's activities and concerns can cause us to grow casual and indifferent toward our blessed relationship with Jesus Christ. God knew our human nature would tend to draw us away from our first love for Jesus (see Rev. 2:4). It happens so gradually that we fail to realize what's happening until our love has grown cold. *No one drifts toward Jesus.*
James Appleby

1. HOW WOULD YOU RATE THE WARMTH OF YOUR LOVE RELATIONSHIP WITH JESUS CHRIST TODAY? CHECK ONE.
   - ☑ a. Hot. I am deeply in love with my Savior.
   - ☑ b. Warm. I feel close to Jesus, but I've been closer.
   - ❑ c. Lukewarm. I go through the motions of faithfulness, but I can't say that I have much passion for Jesus.
   - ❑ d. Cold. I am pretty distant from and indifferent to Christ.

Wherever you find yourself in your love relationship with Jesus Christ, God is reaching out to you. He is inviting you to a deeper experience of the love relationship for which Jesus Christ gave His life. Most of us would have to confess that we need to return to a deeper love for Christ. Fortunately, God loves us too much to let us drift away from Him without attempting to draw us back. That's why He gave us instructions for experiences that can help us remember His blessings. Through these events He guides us to renew a close fellowship with Him and return to our first love.

Of all the ways we can be restored to fellowship with Christ, no experience holds more meaning or emotion for that purpose than the celebration of the Lord's Supper. Different groups call it by different names, like Communion or Holy Eucharist. God isn't as concerned about what we call the celebration as He is that we use the experience to renew our new-covenant relationship with Jesus Christ, our Savior. Probably, the reason you are studying this book is that your church family has chosen to use it to help you prepare for an observance of the Lord's table. Welcome!

2. WHAT NAME DOES YOUR CHURCH USE FOR THE HOLY SUPPER JESUS INSTITUTED ON THE NIGHT BEFORE THE CROSS?
   ☒ a. The Lord's Supper   ☒ b. Communion   ❏ c. Eucharist
   ❏ d. Other: _____

Different churches and Christian traditions use different names for this holy meal. I'll use *Lord's table* to refer to the Lord's Supper, Communion, Eucharist, or another title your church may use.

This devotional guide has been prepared to help you and your church get ready to partake of the Lord's table in a worthy manner. Please participate in the preparations. Each week you will be encouraged to meet with a small group of fellow believers to share, pray, and prepare together. Days 7, 14, 21, and 28 have special activities to guide your small-group session. Make every effort to join your church family during these days of preparation for this very special occasion. I recommend that you cancel or change any conflicts that would prevent your participation.

For the Old Testament sacred assemblies, participants were commanded "not to do any regular work" (Lev. 23:7, NIV; also see vv. 8,21,25, 31,35-36). I recommend that you take the day off from work on the day scheduled for the Lord's table. Give the entire day to the Lord as a sacrifice and thank offering. Another characteristic of the sacred assemblies in the Bible was that all of the people who could understand were expected to attend. Plan now to join your church in this special sacred assembly.

3. WHICH OF THE FOLLOWING WILL YOU AGREE TO DO FOR THE CELEBRATION OF THE LORD'S TABLE? CHECK ALL THAT APPLY.
   ☒ a. I plan to attend the Lord's table service.
   ☐ b. I will need to take a day off from work to attend. — ∅work on Sunday
   ☒ c. I will take time daily to complete these devotional messages in preparation for the Lord's table.
   ☒ d. I will attend the small-group sessions in preparation for the Lord's table. (Will be skipping one)

Throughout this study you may realize that you must do something in response to an activity. For instance, you may realize that you need to rearrange your work schedule to be free for the Lord's table celebration. You may need to make a visit or a phone call. You may need to perform an act of service. I've prepared a space for you to keep a to-do list.

4. IF YOU NEED TO DO SOMETHING TO ARRANGE YOUR SCHEDULE TO PARTICIPATE IN THE LORD'S TABLE, WRITE THE ACTION ON "MY PREPARATIONS" LIST ON PAGE 127.

Each day I will ask you to pray. This is not just a religious activity. It's your <u>invitation to interact with your Lord</u>. Please take advantage of these invitations to talk to Him. Your personal prayer times may prove to be the most significant and meaningful parts of this study. The prayer times will be set off from regular text like the one below.

AS YOU BEGIN YOUR PREPARATIONS FOR THE LORD'S TABLE, PRAY AND ASK THE LORD TO FOCUS YOUR ATTENTION ON THE CROSS AND THE SACRIFICE OF HIS SON, JESUS, FOR YOUR SINS. ASK HIM TO GUIDE YOU IN YOUR PREPARATIONS SO THAT YOU WILL BE A WORTHY GUEST AT THE SUPPER. TAKE TIME TO PRAY NOW.

Day 2 ~ The Wounded Savior

"Worthy is the Lamb who was slain
to receive power, and riches, and wisdom,
and strength, and honor, and glory, and blessing!"

Revelation 5:12, KJV

*B*efore we begin our focus on the meaning of the Lord's table, I want to share with you a testimony of what God can do with a people who celebrate it in a worthy manner. Let this story build your faith and increase your prayers for your own church.

In *The Key to the Missionary Problem* Andrew Murray described a moving encounter with Christ that Count Nicholas Ludwig von Zinzendorf had in a Dusseldorf museum. A painter had painted a picture of the suffering Christ. The painter himself had been so affected by Christ's love for him that he wanted to do something for Christ. He wanted to paint a picture of Jesus that would convey his love for his Savior. Below the picture he wrote the words:

> *All this I did for thee,*
> *What hast thou done for Me?*

When Zinzendorf saw the painting and read the words, "his heart was touched. He felt as if he could not answer the question. He turned away more determined than ever to spend his life in the service of his Lord. The vision of that face never left him. Christ's love became the constraining power of his life. 'I have,' he exclaimed, 'but one passion—'tis He, and He only.' It was His dying love that fitted Christ for the work God had given Him as the Saviour of men. It was the dying love of Christ mastering his life that fitted Zinzendorf for the work he had to do."[1]

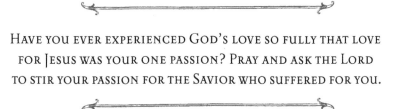

HAVE YOU EVER EXPERIENCED GOD'S LOVE SO FULLY THAT LOVE
FOR JESUS WAS YOUR ONE PASSION? PRAY AND ASK THE LORD
TO STIR YOUR PASSION FOR THE SAVIOR WHO SUFFERED FOR YOU.

Zinzendorf returned home to provide spiritual leadership for a group of about three hundred people who had moved to his estate to escape religious persecution. Most were Moravians, a religious group related to the martyr John Hus, but the refugees included Lutherans, followers of Calvin and Zwingli, Anabaptists, and others. In the spring of 1727 internal conflict was about to destroy the religious community. Zinzendorf and three other elders drew up a covenant of brotherly union that described the way these Christians would live together. It recognized their differences but insisted on brotherly love and unity in the body of Christ.

On May 12, 1727, the entire community repented of their divisions, were reconciled with their brethren, and entered a covenant to live in harmony to honor their Lord. Murray quoted from their diary account of that day: "The Brethren all promised, one by one, that they would be the Saviour's true followers. Self-will, self-love, disobedience—they bade these farewell. They would seek to be poor in spirit; no one was to seek his own profit before that of others; everyone would give himself to be taught by the Holy Spirit."[2]

God began to bind this body of believers together in love and unity. On August 13, 1727, they had a significant encounter with their Savior at a Lord's Supper observance.

On Sunday, 10th, Pastor Rothe was leading the afternoon meeting at Herrnhut, when he was overpowered and fell on his face before God. The whole congregation bowed under the sense of God's presence, and continued in prayer till midnight. He invited the congregation to the Holy Supper on the next Wednesday, the 13th.

As it was the first communion since the new fellowship, it was resolved to be specially strict with it, and to make use of it "to lead the souls deeper into the death of Christ, into which they had been baptized." The leaders visited every member, seeking in great love to lead them to true heart-searching. In the evening of Tuesday, at the preparation service, several passed from death to life, and the whole community was deeply touched.

> On the Wednesday morning all went to Berthelsdorf. On the way thither, any who had felt estranged from each other afresh bound themselves together. During the singing of the first hymn a wicked man was powerfully convicted. The presentation of the new communicants touched every heart, and when the hymn was sung it could hardly be recognized whether there was more singing or weeping. Several brethren prayed, specially pleading that, as exiles out of the house of bondage, they knew not what to do, that they desired to be kept free from separation and sectarianism, and besought the Lord to reveal to them the true nature of His Church, so that they might walk unspotted before Him, might not abide alone but be made fruitful. We asked that we might do nothing contrary to the oath of loyalty we had taken to Him, nor in the very least sin against His law of love. We asked that He would keep us in the saving power of His grace, and not allow a single soul to be drawn away to itself and its own merits from that Blood-and-Cross Theology, on which our salvation depends. We celebrated the Lord's Supper with hearts at once bowed down and lifted up. We went home, each of us in great measure lifted up beyond himself, spending this and the following days in great quiet and peace, and learning to love.

Among those present in the church when the communion was held were a number of children. One writes: "I cannot attribute the great revival among the children to anything else but that wonderful outpouring of the Holy Spirit on the communion assembly. The Spirit breathed in power on old and young. Everywhere they were heard, sometimes at night in the field, beseeching the Saviour to pardon their sins and make them His own. The Spirit of grace had indeed been poured out."[3]

Following that encounter with Christ, the Moravian Brethren were possessed by a zeal for missions. They began a 24-hour prayer watch for the causes of the kingdom, which continued for more than 100 years. During the following 25 years they sent out more than one hundred missionaries.

Some of those missionaries met John Wesley on a boat bound for America in 1735. In them Wesley saw a personal faith in Christ, a love for Christ, and a calm assurance that were different from his own. When he returned to London, Wesley came to personal faith in Christ in a Moravian chapel at Aldersgate. He went from there a different man and led the Evangelical Revival (the First Great Awakening) in England. Even William Carey, known as the father of modern missions, was greatly influenced toward missions by the testimonies of these Moravian missionaries.

In *The Key to the Missionary Problem* Murray quoted Reverend P. de Schweinitz, who summed up the work of the Moravian Brethren.

1. AS YOU READ THE FOLLOWING DESCRIPTION OF MORAVIAN MISSIONS, LOOK FOR THE THING THAT MOTIVATED AND INSPIRED THE MORAVIANS' WORK. UNDERLINE THEIR BATTLE CRY.

Even today [1901] the Moravians have for every fifty-eight communicants in the home churches a missionary in the foreign field, and for every member in the home churches they have more than two members in the congregation gathered from among the heathen. ... Now, what was the incentive for foreign missionary work which has produced such results? While acknowledging, the supreme authority of the great commission, the Moravian Brethren have ever emphasized as their chief incentive the inspiring truth drawn from Isaiah 53:10-12: making our Lord's suffering the spur to all their activity. From that prophecy they drew their missionary battle-cry: "To win for the Lamb that was slain, the reward of His sufferings." We feel that we must compensate Him in some way for the awful sufferings which He endured in working out our salvation. The only way we can reward Him is by bringing souls to Him. When we bring Him souls, that is compensation for the travail of His soul. In no other way can we so effectively bring the suffering Saviour the reward of His passion as by missionary labour, whether we go ourselves or enable others to go. Get this burning thought of "personal love for the Saviour who redeemed me" into the hearts of all Christians, and you have the most powerful incentive that can be had for missionary effort. Oh, if we could make this missionary problem a personal one! if we could fill the hearts of the people with a personal love for this Saviour who died for them, the indifference of Christendom would disappear, and the kingdom of Christ would appear.[4]

2. COPY THE BATTLE CRY OF THE MORAVIANS BELOW.

To win for the Lamb that was Slain, the reward of His sufferings.

3. WHICH OF THE FOLLOWING BEST DESCRIBES THE THOUGHT THAT MOTIVATED AND INSPIRED THE MORAVIANS TO SERVE CHRIST?
   - ❏ a. They read Christ's commands and served from a sense of duty to the commands.
   - ❏ b. Their spiritual leaders, like Zinzendorf, made them feel guilty and ashamed if they did not serve.
   - ☒ c. Their love for the wounded Savior, who died to redeem them, gave them a zeal to serve Him.

If only all believers would see Christ as our wounded Savior in the same way! These men and women were prepared to give their all, even their lives, because of their love for Christ. Paul described this motivation this way: "Christ's love compels us, since we have reached this conclusion: One died for all, then all died. And He died for all so that those who live should no longer live for themselves, but for the One who died for them and was raised" (2 Cor. 5:14-15). At a picture gallery in Germany, God instilled in Count Zinzendorf a personal love for the wounded and suffering Savior. His life and ministry were forever changed as he resigned from his governmental duties to work with God's people on his estate. At the Lord's table those Moravian Brethren had a moving encounter with the wounded Savior, and they were never the same. I pray that the upcoming Lord's table experience will be just as moving for you and your church.

4. IN THE FOLLOWING SONG JESUS ASKS SOME QUESTIONS. AS YOU
READ OR SING THIS SONG, UNDERLINE THE FOUR QUESTIONS.

I Gave My Life for Thee

Frances R. Havergal

I gave My life for thee,
My precious blood I shed,
That thou might'st ransomed be,
And quickened from the dead;
I gave, I gave My life for thee,
What hast thou giv'n for Me?

I suffered much for thee,
More than thy tongue can tell,
Of bitt'rest agony,
To rescue thee from hell;
I've borne, I've borne it all for thee,
What hast thou borne for Me?

My Father's house of light,
My glory-circled throne,
I left, for earthly night,
For wand'rings sad and lone;
I left, I left it all for thee,
Hast thou left aught for Me?

And I have brought to thee,
Down from My home above,
Salvation full and free,
My pardon and My love;
I bring, I bring rich gifts to thee,
What hast thou brought to Me?

PRAY THAT GOD WILL GIVE YOU AND MEMBERS
OF YOUR CHURCH A DEEPER LOVE FOR YOUR WOUNDED SAVIOR
THAN YOU HAVE EVER KNOWN BEFORE. OVER THE NEXT FEW
WEEKS LISTEN TO THE QUESTION "ALL THIS I DID FOR YOU.
WHAT HAVE YOU DONE FOR ME?"

1. Andrew Murray, *The Key to the Missionary Problem* (New York: American Tract Society, 1901), 45.

2. Ibid., 47.

3. Ibid., 49–50.

4. Reverend P. de Schweinitz, in Murray, *The Key*, 36–37.

Day 3 ~ The Last Supper

"When the hour came, He reclined at the table, and the apostles with Him. Then He said to them, 'I have fervently desired to eat this Passover with you before I suffer.'"

Luke 22:14-15

$\mathcal{L}$et me take you on a mental journey back in time. Go with me to Jerusalem the day before Jesus died on the cross. Jerusalem is filled with people who have come to celebrate a great festival—the Passover and the Feast of Unleavened Bread. People crowd the streets. Worshipers chant psalms of praise as they remember the miraculous way God brought Israel out of Egypt. An elder from each family or group takes a young lamb to the temple. After three loud blasts from the silver trumpets, the lambs are killed. Blood from each lamb is sprinkled at the altar. Then the elders head home to roast their Passover lambs for the evening meal.

Peter and John are there. They are preparing for Jesus to celebrate the Passover with His twelve disciples. In an upper room a table is set with bitter herbs, unleavened bread, and four cups of wine. The roasted lamb is brought to the table as the twelve disciples gather with Jesus. Little do the disciples know that this will be the last Passover meal they will eat with their Master.

1. READ LUKE 22:14-20 IN YOUR BIBLE AND ANSWER THE FOLLOWING QUESTIONS.

the cup ~~not until the kingdom of God comes.~~

    a. When will Jesus eat another meal and drink of "the fruit
       of the vine" with His disciples?

the meal ~~Not until it is~~ *fulfilled in the kingdom of God.*

    b. What does the bread of the supper represent? _His body_ *broken*

    c. What does the cup (wine or juice) represent? _His blood_ *shed*

Jesus will eat the next meal and drink of the fruit of the vine when God's kingdom comes—when it reaches its fulfillment. The bread represents the Lord's body that was broken on the cross for us. In a similar way, the wine represents His blood that was shed for us. It is the blood of a new covenant between God and His people.

    The original Passover meal was a time to remember God's deliverance of Israel from bondage in Egypt. Jesus established the Lord's Supper as a time to remember Him and His sacrifice to deliver people from their sins. He said, "Do this in remembrance of Me" (v. 19).

    The day after the last supper, Jesus went to the cross to give His body and blood as a sacrifice for the sin of the world.

   2. PAUSE TO REMEMBER JESUS AND HIS SACRIFICE ON THE CROSS
     OF CALVARY. READ OR SING THE FOLLOWING HYMN.

At the Cross

Isaac Watts

Alas, and did my Saviour bleed,
And did my Sov'reign die?
Would He devote that sacred head
For sinners such as I?

Was it for crimes that I had done
He groaned upon the tree?
Amazing pity, grace unknown,
And love beyond degree!

Well might the sun in darkness hide,
And shut his glories in,
When Christ the mighty Maker died
For man, the creature's sin.

But drops of grief can ne'er repay
The debt of love I owe:
Here, Lord, I give myself away,
'Tis all that I can do!

On that Good Friday Jesus gave His life as "the Lamb of God, who takes away the sin of the world" (John 1:29). By His payment of a death penalty for my sins and yours, we are now set free from bondage to sin. Your celebration of the Lord's table as a sacred assembly will be a time to remember Jesus and His loving sacrifice for you.

EXPRESS YOUR LOVE AND THANKS TO JESUS IN PRAYER.
ASK HIM TO HELP YOU REMEMBER HIM IN A WORTHY WAY.
ON A SEPARATE SHEET OF PAPER WRITE A FEW WORDS
OF YOUR PRAYER OF THANKSGIVING. IF YOU PREFER,
WRITE A POEM OF GRATITUDE TO HIM.

---

3. TAKE TIME AWAY FROM YOUR OTHER ACTIVITIES TODAY TO MEDITATE ON THE CROSS AND JESUS' SACRIFICE OF HIS BODY AND BLOOD FOR YOU. USE THE WORDS OF THIS HYMN TO FOCUS ON JESUS' SACRIFICE.

When I Survey the Wondrous Cross
Isaac Watts

When I survey the wondrous cross,
On which the Prince of glory died,
My richest gain I count but loss,
And pour contempt
on all my pride.

See, from His head,
His hands, His feet,
Sorrow and love flow mingled down;
Did e'er such love and sorrow meet,
Or thorns compose so rich a crown?

Forbid it, Lord, that I should boast,
Save in the death of Christ, my God;
All the vain things
that charm me most,
I sacrifice them to His blood.

Were the whole realm
of nature mine,
That were a present far too small;
Love so amazing, so divine,
Demands my soul, my life, my all.

Day 4 ~ The Wedding Supper of the Lamb

"Let us be glad, rejoice, and give Him glory,
because the marriage of the Lamb has come,
and His wife has prepared herself. ...
'Blessed are those invited
to the marriage feast of the Lamb!'"

Revelation 19:7-9

In Leviticus 23 God prescribed festivals and celebrations as sacred assemblies for His people. Each one had divine purposes to rekindle the love and reverence of God's people for Him. In writing to the church, Paul said Israel's religious festivals, New Moon celebrations, and Sabbaths "are a shadow of the things that were to come; the reality, however, is found in Christ" (Col. 2:17, NIV).

For instance, some believe Jesus was actually born during the Feast of Tabernacles, when shepherds were more likely to be in the fields at night. If this was the case, just as Israel celebrated God's coming to dwell in a tabernacle in the days of Moses, Jesus came to live among us as Immanuel—"God is with us" (Matt. 1:23). The feast was a shadow of the reality that was in Christ. Others believe the fulfillment of the Feast of Tabernacles will come with Christ's kingdom rule in eternity. Whenever the fulfillment takes place, we can rejoice in the reality that Christ came to dwell among us and now lives in us by His Holy Spirit.

At the time of the Feast of Passover, Jesus was revealed as the Lamb of God who was slain to take away the sin of the world. Christ's sacrifice became the ultimate reality of deliverance for God's people. At Pentecost (the Feast of Firstfruits) the Holy Spirit came on the disciples, and the firstfruits of the church were harvested as three thousand came to faith in Christ in a single day (see Acts 2). The fulfillment of the Feast of Trumpets will be Jesus' second coming, when the final trumpet will sound to call the elect home to heaven. The Day of Atonement is a shadow of judgment day, when we will all appear before the judgment seat of Christ. Each shadow points to a reality in Christ.

1. MATCH THE SACRED ASSEMBLY (SHADOW) ON THE LEFT WITH THE FULFILLMENT (REALITY) ON THE RIGHT.

_C_ 1. Feast of Passover   a. Judgment day *1,000 yr Kingdom rule?*

_d_ 2. Feast of Pentecost   b. Jesus' ~~birth as Immanuel~~

_e_ 3. Feast of Trumpets   c. Jesus' death as the Lamb of God

_a_ 4. Day of Atonement   d. Firstfruits of the church

_b_ 5. Feast of Tabernacles   e. Christ's second coming

(Answers: 1-c, 2-d, 3-e, 4-a, 5-b)

These sacred assemblies were shadows of realities that are found in Christ. In a similar way, the Lord's Supper is a shadow of something to come— the wedding supper of the Lamb!

2. READ ABOUT THE WEDDING SUPPER OF THE LAMB AND UNDERLINE WORDS THAT DESCRIBE THE PREPARATIONS OF THE CHURCH—THE BRIDE (OR WIFE) OF CHRIST. WHAT WILL SHE HAVE DONE?

> Let us be glad, rejoice, and give Him glory,
> because the marriage of the Lamb has come,
> and His wife [bride, NIV] has prepared herself.
> She was permitted to wear fine linen, bright and pure.
> For the fine linen represents the righteous acts of the saints.
> (Rev. 19:7-8).

The bride will have already "prepared herself" (v. 7). She will be clean and dressed in fine linen—"the righteous acts of the saints" (v. 8).

3. Based on your knowledge of the Christian church at large (all of God's redeemed people), would you say the bride of Christ is clean, dressed, and ready for the wedding supper of the Lamb? Is she clean and pure? ❑ Yes ❑ No

Why or why not? _____

_____

_____

Probably, most Christians would sadly have to admit that the bride of Christ is far from ready. She is too impure, unclean, and unrighteous to be an acceptable bride for God's only Son, Jesus. The bride, however, needs to be ready for His return at any time.

Do you remember that Jesus said He would not eat the Passover or drink the fruit of the vine again until these acts find fulfillment in the kingdom of God (see Luke 22:16,18)? The wedding supper of the Lamb is that fulfillment in the coming kingdom of God. What a special day that will be for the bride of Christ—the church. The angel said, "Blessed are those invited to the marriage feast of the Lamb!"

The Lord's table is not just a time to look back at the cross. It is also a time to look forward to the Lord's return for His bride. Paul said, "As often as you eat this bread and drink the cup, you proclaim the Lord's death until He comes" (1 Cor. 11:26). As you prepare for the celebration of the Lord's table, you will look back to remember the cross. You will also want to prepare yourself to be ready for your future as the pure bride of Christ.

By looking back at the last supper and the cross, you will grow in your love and appreciation of Christ for the sacrifice He made for you. By looking forward, you will realize that you need to get ready for the wedding supper of the Lamb.

As Christ's bride, we want to be clean and pleasing to Him. The Lord's table provides a regular opportunity to prepare ourselves. We need to be right with God and with one another. We need to be clean and pure. We need to be dressed in righteous acts.

4. HOW WOULD YOU DESCRIBE YOUR ATTENTION TO AND PREPARATIONS FOR CHRIST'S RETURN AND THE WEDDING SUPPER OF THE LAMB? CHECK THE STATEMENT THAT BEST DESCRIBES YOU.

☒ a. I regularly think about His return and seek to keep myself clean and pure for that day. I want to be ready.

❑ b. I really don't think much about His return. I'm not ready.

❑ c. I'm somewhere between a and b.

5. READ OR SING THIS SONG TEXT AND REFLECT ON YOUR SAVIOR. THINK ABOUT MEETING YOUR BRIDEGROOM—THE GLORIOUS KING.

"Man of Sorrows," What a Name

Philip P. Bliss

"Man of sorrows!" what a name
For the Son of God who came
Ruined sinners to reclaim!
Hallelujah, what a Savior!

Bearing shame and scoffing rude,
In my place condemned He stood,
Seal'd my pardon with His blood;
Hallelujah, what a Savior!

Lifted up was He to die,
"It is finished," was His cry;
Now in heav'n exalted high,
Hallelujah, what a Savior!

When He comes,
our glorious King,
All His ransomed home to bring,
Then anew this song we'll sing,
Hallelujah, what a Savior!

IMAGINE WHAT THE WEDDING SUPPER OF THE LAMB WILL BE LIKE. MEDITATE ON WHAT KIND OF BRIDE WILL BE PLEASING TO JESUS. ASK THE LORD TO BEGIN REVEALING TO YOU ANYTHING YOU NEED TO DO TO GET YOUR LIFE IN LINE WITH HIM AND HIS WILL. AS THE LORD BEGINS REVEALING THESE THINGS, WRITE THEM ON "MY PREPARATIONS" LIST ON PAGE 127. THEN TAKE THE ACTIONS NEEDED.

Day 5 ~ The Divine Invitation

"Tell those who are invited:
Look, I've prepared my dinner; ...
and everything is ready.
Come to the wedding banquet."

Matthew 22:4

In Matthew 22:1-14 Jesus told a parable about His coming kingdom. A parable is a simple story that reveals spiritual truth. Jesus described a king who invited people to the wedding banquet for his son: "Tell those who are invited: Look, I've prepared my dinner; … and everything is ready. Come to the wedding banquet" (Matt. 22:4). Sadly, those who were first invited refused to come. The king in the parable sent his army to destroy them and burn their city. What a tragedy.

Next the king sent his servants to invite anyone they could find: "'The banquet is ready, but those who were invited were not worthy. Therefore, go to where the roads exit the city and invite everyone you find to the banquet.' So those slaves went out on the roads and gathered everyone they found, both evil and good. The wedding banquet was filled with guests" (Matt. 22:8-10).

This parable illustrates the wedding supper of the Lamb. God is preparing a great wedding banquet for His Son, Jesus Christ. He is inviting people to come. Those who come to faith in Jesus as Savior and Lord will be welcome guests.

? 1. Those who come to faith in Jesus Christ are the bride.

23 *2. The guests are not chosen but general invitation both evil + good*

1. READ THE FOLLOWING INVITATIONS AND CIRCLE THE WORD *COME* EACH TIME IT OCCURS.

  - "Come to Me, all of you who are weary and burdened, and I will give you rest. All of you, take up My yoke and learn from Me, because I am gentle and humble in heart, and you will find rest for yourselves. For My yoke is easy and My burden is light" (Matt. 11:28-30).
  - "The time is fulfilled, and the kingdom of God has come near. Repent and believe in the good news!" (Mark 1:14-15).
  - "If anyone is thirsty, he should come to Me and drink! The one who believes in Me, as the Scripture has said, will have streams of living water flow from deep within him" (John 7:37-38).
  - "Both the Spirit and the bride say, 'Come!' Anyone who hears should say, 'Come!' And the one who is thirsty should come. Whoever desires should take the living water as a gift" (Rev. 22:17).

Each person must choose whether to come to the Lord and attend His wedding feast.

2. HAVE YOU MADE PLANS TO ATTEND? HAVE YOU PLACED YOUR FAITH IN JESUS AND ACCEPTED THE REDEMPTION HE PROVIDED FOR YOU THROUGH HIS DEATH ON THE CROSS? HAVE YOU COME TO JESUS FOR HIS LIVING WATER? HAVE YOU RECEIVED THE FREE GIFT OF ETERNAL LIFE?　☒ Yes　❑ No　❑ Not yet

Those who have said yes to Jesus' invitation are invited to the marriage supper in eternity. As we look forward to that event, we celebrate the Lord's table in remembrance of Him. If you have made the spiritual preparations, you are invited to the Lord's table. Symbolically, God sends the word to us: "Tell those who are invited: Look, I've prepared my dinner; … and everything is ready. Come to the wedding banquet" (Matt. 22:4). For His children—Jesus' disciples—God has a similar invitation to the Lord's table. He invites you to come and be nourished as you remember Jesus until He comes again.

3. AS YOU READ THE FOLLOWING MEDITATION BY ANDREW MURRAY, THINK ABOUT THE GLORIOUS FACT THAT YOU ARE INVITED TO DINE AT THE TABLE OF YOUR LORD JESUS CHRIST.

Let the King of Heaven and Earth say to you, "Come to the wedding banquet" (AM). In honor of His Son He has prepared a great supper. He has invited you to the great festival of His Divine love. He is prepared to receive and honor you as a guest and friend. He will feed you with His heavenly food.

O my brothers and sisters, you also have received this heavenly invitation. You have been asked to eat with the King of Glory! Embrace and be occupied with this honor.

Glorious invitation! I think of the banquet itself and what it has cost the great God to prepare it. To prepare for man upon this accursed earth a banquet of heavenly food—that cost Him much. That cost Him the life and blood of His Son to take away the curse and to open up to them the right and the access to heavenly blessings. Nothing less than the body and the blood of the Son of God could give life to lost men. Take time to ponder the wonders of this royal banquet.

I think of the invitation. It is as free, as wide as it could be, "without money and without price" (AM). The poorest and the most unworthy are called to it. It is an urgent and loving invitation. Not less cordial is the love which invites to it, the love which longs after sinners and takes delight in entertaining and blessing them.

I think of the blessing of the banquet. The dying are fed with the power of a heavenly life. The lost are restored to their places in the Father's house. And those who thirst after God are satisfied with God Himself and with His love.

Glorious invitation! With adoration I receive it, and prepare myself to make use of it. I have read of those who hold themselves excused because they are hindered—one by his merchandise, another by his work, and a third by his domestic happiness. I have heard the voice which has said, "I say unto you, that none of these men which were invited shall taste of My supper" (AM). Because He who invites me is the Holy One, who will not suffer Himself to be mocked, I will prepare myself to lay aside all thoughtlessness, to withdraw myself from the seductions of the world; and with all earnestness to yield obedience to the voice of the heavenly love. I will remain in quiet meditation and in fellowship with the children of God, to keep myself free from all needless anxiety about the world, and as an invited guest, to meet my God with real hunger and quiet joy. He Himself will not withhold from me His help in this work (LT, pp. 15–18).

4. HAVE YOU EVER BEFORE STOPPED TO THINK THIS SERIOUSLY ABOUT GOD'S INVITATION FOR YOU TO COME TO COMMUNION WITH HIM? ☒ Yes ❑ No

5. HOW WOULD YOU DESCRIBE YOUR PREVIOUS INVITATIONS TO THE LORD'S TABLE? CHECK ANY RESPONSES THAT APPLY TO YOUR PAST EXPERIENCE.
   ❑ a. I've never stopped to think that God Himself is inviting me to the Lord's table.
   ☒ b. I've been awed many times by the realization that the Creator of the universe has invited me to His banquet.
   ❑ c. I just thought of the Lord's table as a church event to which I was invited if I wanted to come.
   ❑ d. Sometimes I've chosen not to attend because I had a conflict in my schedule. I didn't think very seriously about it.

6. WITH SUCH A WONDERFUL INVITATION, DO YOU NEED TO CANCEL OTHER PLANS SO THAT YOU CAN PARTICIPATE IN THIS VERY SPECIAL SACRED ASSEMBLY OF YOUR CHURCH? ❑ Yes ☒ No

7. IF SO, WHAT DO YOU NEED TO DO? WRITE IT ON "MY PREPARATIONS" LIST ON PAGE 127.

If you have a conflict, very seriously consider rearranging your schedule so that you can be present with the rest of your church family for this sacred assembly. As one who has been redeemed, you are invited by Christ Himself.

CONCLUDE TODAY'S LESSON BY READING AND PRAYING
THE FOLLOWING PRAYER BY ANDREW MURRAY.
AS YOU PRAY, UNDERLINE STATEMENTS OR THOUGHTS
THAT ARE ESPECIALLY MEANINGFUL TO YOU.

Eternal God, I have received the good tidings that there is room also for me at the table of Your Son. O God of all grace, with grateful thanks I receive Your invitation. I hunger for Your bread, O Lord. My soul thirsts for God. My flesh and my heart cry out for the Living God. When will I enter and appear before the face of God?

Lord, graciously bestow upon me this next week a real blessing in the way of preparation. Let the sight of my sinfulness humble me deeply and take away from me all hope in myself. Let the sight of Your grace again encourage me and fill me with confidence and gladness. Stir up within me a mighty desire for the Bridegroom, for the precious Jesus, without whom there could be no feast. And may I be filled with the thought that I have an invitation to eat bread in the house of my God with his only-begotten and well-beloved Son. Lord, grant this for Jesus' sake.

Lord Jesus, You have taught me: "God is a spirit, and they that worship Him must worship Him in spirit and in truth" (AM). Lord, spiritual worship I cannot bring: but You will bestow Your Spirit upon me. I entreat You, Lord, to grant the working of the Spirit. The blessing of the Supper is a high spiritual blessing. There at the Supper, the invisible God will come very near to us. Only the spiritual mind can enjoy the spiritual blessing. You know how deeply I fail in this receptiveness for a full blessing. But grant, I pray You, that the Holy Spirit may this week dwell and work in me with special power. I will surrender myself for this end to Him and to His guidance, in order that He may overcome in me the spirit of the world and renew my inner life to inherit from my God a new blessing. Lord, let Your Spirit work mightily within me.

And as I thus pray for myself, I pray also for the whole congregation. Grant, Lord, in behalf of all Your children an overflowing outpouring of Your Spirit, in order that this Supper may really be for all of us a time of quickening and renewal of our energies. Amen (LT, pp. 18–20).

Day 6 ~ From Supper to the Cross

"When they arrived at the place called The Skull, they crucified Him there, along with the criminals, one on the right and one on the left."

Luke 23:33

AS WE TURN OUR ATTENTION TO THE CROSS OF CHRIST, PRAY (AND SING, IF YOU LIKE) THE WORDS OF "LEAD ME TO CALVARY" ON PAGE 29.

"Lest I forget ... , lead me to Calvary." In order to remember Him, let's follow Jesus to Calvary.

PAUSE TO PRAY AND ASK GOD TO HELP YOU REMEMBER JESUS AND HIS SUFFERING ON THE CROSS.
WRITE A BRIEF PRAYER BELOW.

Dear Jesus, *You gave the infinite sacrifice for me. You gave Yourself + suffered infinitely. Please give me an ever increasing awareness and gratefulness for You.*

Lead Me to Calvary

Jennie E. Hussey

King of my life, I crown Thee now,
Thine shall the glory be;
Lest I forget Thy
thorn-crowned brow,
Lead me to Calvary.

Show me the tomb
where Thou wast laid,
Tenderly mourned and wept;
Angels in robes of light arrayed
Guarded Thee whilst Thou slept.

Let me like Mary, thro' the gloom,
Come with a gift to Thee;

Show to me now the empty tomb,
Lead me to Calvary.

May I be willing, Lord, to bear
Daily my cross for Thee;
Even Thy cup of grief to share,
Thou has borne all for me.

Refrain
Lest I forget Gethsemane;
Lest I forget Thine agony;
Lest I forget Thy love for me,
Lead me to Calvary.

When Jesus had finished the last supper with His disciples, He began a very determined movement toward the cross. First Jesus crossed the valley and went to the Mount of Olives to a garden area to pray. During this prayer time in Gethsemane Jesus received strength for the final move to the cross. Facing His own greatest temptation, Jesus said to Peter, James, and John, "My soul is swallowed up in sorrow—to the point of death. Remain here and stay awake with Me" (Matt. 26:38). Then three times Jesus prayed, "Father, if You are willing, take this cup away from Me—nevertheless, not My will, but Yours, be done.' Then an angel from heaven appeared to Him, strengthening Him. Being in anguish, He prayed more fervently, and His sweat became like drops of blood falling to the ground" (Luke 22:42-44).

✥ 1. WHICH OF THE FOLLOWING FEELINGS AND EMOTIONS DO YOU THINK JESUS MUST HAVE FELT? CHECK ALL YOU THINK APPLY.

❑ Fear of the pain from the beating, thorns, and nails
❑ Fear of the abuse, ridicule, and shame He would endure
☒ Betrayal by Judas and the religious leaders of God's people
☒ Sorrow and grief for those who would reject Him and His salvation
☒ Hurt and disappointment over the denials of Peter, one of His closest disciples
→ ☒ Isolation from His Father when Jesus would become sin for the world
☒ Loneliness because of the other disciples' desertion
❑ Wonder whether He could humanly endure to the end
☒ Questions about what it would be like to carry the weight of the sin of the world in His own sinless life
☒ Love for His Father that prompted Him to obey
☒ Love for a lost world, knowing that without Him they had no hope, but by His death they could receive salvation
☒ Confidence in His Father's resurrection power
☒ Eagerness to return to heaven

Jesus may have felt all of these emotions that night as He agonized in prayer. You may think of others.

Were You There? Gal 2:20

African-American Spiritual

Were you there when they
crucified my Lord?
Were you there when they
crucified my Lord?

Oh! Sometimes it causes me
to tremble, tremble, tremble.
Were you there when they
crucified my Lord?

The ones in authority misusing their power to abuse One Whom they viewed as weak – Yet He is the Sovereign One of the universe – the Source of all authority. Truly, as Jesus prayed, "they know not what they do."

2. TURN IN YOUR BIBLE AND READ ABOUT JESUS' TRIAL AND CRUCIFIXION IN LUKE 22:63–23:49. AS YOU READ, TRY TO IMAGINE YOU WERE THERE IN THE CROWD WATCHING THESE EVENTS TAKE PLACE. KEEP IN MIND THAT JESUS WAS THE SINLESS SON OF GOD, WHO CAME TO PROVIDE SALVATION TO ALL. WRITE WORDS OR PHRASES BELOW THAT DESCRIBE THE SUFFERING, RIDICULE, AND SHAME HE ENDURED TO PROVIDE FOR YOUR SALVATION.

Purposeful laying down His life – He allowed men (whom He created) to beat Him, mock Him, crucify Him.

Sovereign vulnerability.

Gracious toleration of belligerent ignorance

Rejection by the ones He loved

Contrast of collision of character

The Truth being battered with deceit and implied false accusations.

ON THE LINES BELOW, WRITE A PRAYER OF THANKSGIVING
TO JESUS FOR THE RIDICULE, SHAME, SUFFERING, AND DEATH
HE ENDURED FOR YOU. IF YOU PREFER, WRITE IT
IN THE FORM OF A POEM OR A SONG.

_____

_____

_____

_____

_____

Sunday

Day 7 ~ Group Session 1

OPEN WITH PRAYER

1. Invite volunteers to describe one of their most meaningful experiences participating in the Lord's table.
2. Open in prayer asking the Lord to visit your church with a special experience of His presence, love, and work during the coming month of preparation.

SING/LISTEN

Select a song or hymn that focuses your attention on Christ and His sacrifice on the cross. Sing it together, read the lyrics, or listen to someone sing it live or from a recording.

REVIEW DAYS 1–6

1. What Scripture, statement, idea, testimony, or illustration that you read this week was most significant or meaningful to you and why?
2. What did you learn about the Lord's table this week that was a new insight or a refreshing reminder of the truths about our celebration of the Lord's sacrifice for us?
3. How has your love for Christ been affected by your devotional times this week?
4. How does your experience of preparation for the Lord's table compare to that described in the preface (p. 4) and that of the Moravian Brethren described in day 2 (p. 10)?
5. What was the battle cry of the Moravian Brethren for missions (p. 13)? Why do you think they developed such a passion for winning the lost world to faith in Christ?
6. What motivated the Moravians to serve Christ? (See activity 3, p. 14.)
7. What is the purpose of remembering Christ's death in the Lord's table observance?

8. What is the value of looking ahead to the marriage supper of the Lamb?
9. In what ways are the sacred assemblies prescribed in the Old Testament a shadow of the realities found in Christ? (See day 4, p. 19.)

RESPOND TO THE LORD IN PRAYER

Pray for your group and your church as you prepare for the Lord's table. Pray that the Lord will rekindle your first love for Christ. Pray that He will stir up a fresh passion for prayer and for reaching your world for Christ, beginning in your own city or community.

RESPOND TO LEARNING ACTIVITIES

1. Day 1, activity 1 (p. 7). How would you rate the warmth of your love relationship with Jesus? Has that changed this week?
2. Day 4, activity 3 (p. 21). How prepared is the bride of Christ for the wedding supper? Share your opinion and why.
3. Day 4, activity 4 (p. 22). How would you describe your readiness for the wedding supper?
4. Day 6, activity 1 (p. 30). What feelings or emotions do you think Jesus felt as He prepared for and experienced the cross?

PREPARE FOR THE LORD'S TABLE

1. Discuss your church's schedule for the Lord's table celebration, small-group sessions, and related activities. Encourage everyone to make plans to attend and participate in the preparations.
2. Do others in your church membership need to be encouraged to join the preparations? If so, who will invite them?
3. What do you sense God wants to do in your life and the life of your church as you prepare to celebrate the Lord's table?

PRAY TOGETHER

Invite volunteers to pray brief sentence prayers of thanksgiving to Jesus for the love He demonstrated on the cross.

PREVIEW THE COMING WEEK

Day 8 ~ Broken Body and Shed Blood

"Jesus took bread, blessed and broke it, gave it

to the disciples, and said, 'Take and eat it; this is

My body.' Then He took a cup, and after

giving thanks, He gave it to them and said,

'Drink from it, all of you. For this is

My blood that establishes the covenant;

it is shed for many for the forgiveness of sins.'"

Matthew 26:26-28

The Lord's table provides a powerful symbol of the sacrifice Jesus made to provide for our forgiveness. Let's reflect on the broken body and shed blood symbolized in the bread and the wine: "On the night when He was betrayed, the Lord Jesus took bread, gave thanks, broke it, and said, 'This is My body, which is for you. Do this in remembrance of Me.' In the same way He also took the cup, after supper, and said, 'This cup is the new covenant in My blood. Do this, as often as you drink it, in remembrance of Me.' For as often as you eat this bread and drink the cup, you proclaim the Lord's death until He comes" (1 Cor. 11:23-26).

When Jesus was born in Bethlehem, an angel appeared to some shepherds and proclaimed, "Don't be afraid, for look, I proclaim to you good news of great joy that will be for all the people: today a Savior, who is Messiah the Lord, was born for you in the city of David" (Luke 2:10-11). Jesus came to be our Savior, to save people from their sins (see Matt. 1:21). But because of our sin and God's justice, the only way our salvation could be purchased was by the shedding of Jesus' blood: "Without the shedding of blood there is no forgiveness" (Heb. 9:22).

1. IN EACH SCRIPTURE UNDERLINE WHAT CHRIST DID FOR US THROUGH HIS BLOOD. I'VE UNDERLINED THE FIRST ONE FOR YOU.
   • "Be on guard for yourselves and for all the flock, among whom the Holy Spirit has appointed you as overseers, to shepherd the church of God, which He purchased with His own blood" (Acts 20:28).
   • "Since we have now been declared righteous by His blood, we will be saved through Him from wrath" (Rom. 5:9).
   • "Now in Christ Jesus, you who were far away have been brought near by the blood of the Messiah" (Eph. 2:13).
   • "God was pleased to have all His fullness dwell in Him, and through Him to reconcile everything to Himself by making peace through the blood of His cross" (Col. 1:19-20).
   • "How much more will the blood of the Messiah, who through the eternal Spirit offered Himself without blemish to God, cleanse our consciences from dead works to serve the living God?" (Heb. 9:14).
   • "If we walk in the light as He Himself is in the light, we have fellowship with one another, and the blood of Jesus His Son cleanses us from all sin" (1 John 1:7).
   • "To Him who loves us and has set us free from our sins by his blood ..." (Rev. 1:5).

By shedding His blood, Jesus accomplished the following.
1. He bought the church.
2. He justified us (declared us righteous).
3. He brought us near.
4. He made peace between God and us.
5. He cleansed our consciences from acts that lead to death.
6. He purified us from all sin.
7. He freed us from our sins.

2. READ OR SING THE FOLLOWING HYMN AND MEDITATE ON THE POWER IN THE BLOOD THAT WAS SHED FOR YOU. UNDERLINE THE THINGS CHRIST'S BLOOD CAN ACCOMPLISH. I'VE UNDERLINED ONE FOR YOU.

There Is Power in the Blood

Lewis E. Jones

Would you be free from
the burden of sin?
There's pow'r in the blood,
pow'r in the blood;
Would you o'er evil a victory win?
There's wonderful pow'r
in the blood.

Would you be free from
your passion and pride?
There's pow'r in the blood,
pow'r in the blood;
Come for a cleansing
to Calvary's tide;
There's wonderful pow'r
in the blood.

Would you be whiter,
much whiter than snow?
There's pow'r in the blood,
pow'r in the blood;
Sin stains are lost in
its life-giving flow;
There's wonderful pow'r
in the blood.

Would you do service
for Jesus your King?
There's pow'r in the blood,
pow'r in the blood;
Would you live daily
His praises to sing?
There's wonderful pow'r
in the blood.

Now I'm going to guide you through an activity that may seem rather childish. Please humble yourself and do it anyway. One person initially didn't want to do this assignment because of its simplicity, but she finally decided to do it. Later she told me that it had a great impact on her. When she came to the Lord's table, the meaning of Christ's shed blood had taken on a much deeper meaning. Take a moment to be like a child again.

3. To help you more clearly understand the Lord's suffering, draw blood on the picture of Christ on this page. If possible, use a red pencil, pen, or crayon. Draw the blood—

- on His head, where the crown of thorns was placed;
- on His hands and feet, where the nails were driven;
- on His sides and shoulders, where the whips on His back drew blood;
- on His side, where the spear was placed to determine whether He was dead;
- on the ground, where the blood fell.

Didn't Jesus demonstrate a great love for you and for me on that cross?

4. How would you describe the love you feel for Jesus now? Check the statement that best describes your love. If these responses are not adequate, write your own.

☒ a. I'm humbled and moved to tears when I think Jesus loved a sinner like me that much.

❑ b. I know in my head He loved me, but I'm still having trouble feeling that love in my heart.

❑ c. I wish He were physically present so that I could give Him a hug.

❑ d. Even though I know Jesus did all that for me, somehow I still don't sense His love in a real way.

❑ e. Other: _____

_____

You might have responded in any one of the ways suggested above. When we really grasp the price Jesus paid to be our Savior, words can never adequately express the love we should have for Him. I pray that you will come to a deep, real, and personal experience of Christ's love. Perhaps through this study and your experience at the Lord's table, Jesus Himself will clearly reveal His love to you so that you will experientially know your Savior deeply loves you. Lord Jesus, make it so.

In a sense Jesus speaks to us from the cross, saying, "I loved you this much!" Pray and thank Him for His love and the sacrifice of His life for you, for shedding His blood for you. Tell Him how much you love Him for what He has done. If you prefer, write a brief statement or poem to Him expressing your love.

God of life, You chose to die
Shedding Your life, and
Dispersing Your love.
Your heart was pierced for the sake of mine.
I love You now, O Savior Devine.

Day 9 ~ Examine Yourself

"Whoever eats the bread or drinks the cup of the
Lord in an unworthy way will be guilty of sin
against the body and blood of the Lord.
So a man should examine himself; in this way
he should eat of the bread and drink of the cup."

1 Corinthians 11:27-28

The Lord's table is a time to look back and remember what Jesus did for us on the cross. It is also a time to look forward with anticipation of His return for His bride—the church. Before we come to the table, we should prepare ourselves. When Paul wrote to the Corinthian church about the Lord's table, he sent a word of correction because the believers were partaking of the supper in an unworthy manner. As we prepare for the supper, we need to follow Paul's instructions so that we will be acceptable guests at the Lord's table.

1. READ PAUL'S INSTRUCTIONS FOR SELF-EXAMINATION. UNDERLINE WHAT PAUL SAID ABOUT THE CONSEQUENCES OF EATING IN AN UNWORTHY MANNER AND BRINGING JUDGMENT ON YOURSELF. WHAT HAD HAPPENED TO MANY AMONG THE CHURCH?

"Whoever eats the bread or drinks the cup of the Lord in an unworthy way will be guilty of <u>sin against the body and blood of the Lord</u>. So a man should examine himself; in this way he should eat of the bread and drink of the cup. For whoever eats and drinks without recognizing the body, <u>eats and drinks judgment on himself</u>. This is why <u>many are sick and ill among you, and many have fallen</u>

asleep. If we were properly evaluating ourselves, we would not be judged, but when we are judged, we are <u>disciplined by the Lord, so that we may not be condemned with the world</u>" (1 Cor. 11:27-32).

Paul explained the danger of partaking in an unworthy manner. Some were weak and sick, and others had died ("fallen asleep," v. 30). He went on to explain that we can either judge ourselves or come under the Lord's judgment. This is one reason I've written this book for you. I don't want you to go the way of the Corinthians and treat the Lord's table casually. I don't want you to suffer the consequences of the Lord's discipline and judgment.

Last week you read Jesus' parable about the wedding banquet. When those who had been invited to the banquet refused to come, the king sent his servants into the streets to invite everyone they could find to the banquet. But "when the king came in to view the guests, he saw a man there who was not dressed for a wedding. So he said to him, 'Friend, how did you get in here without wedding clothes?' The man was speechless. Then the king told the attendants, 'Tie him up hand and foot, and throw him into the outer darkness, where there will be weeping and gnashing of teeth'" (Matt. 22:11-13).

Those who don't have a saving faith relationship with Jesus Christ are not prepared for the wedding supper of the Lamb. They are not wearing the proper wedding clothes. Because the Lord's table is a time to remember what Jesus did for you in providing for your salvation, this relationship with Him is required in order to be a worthy guest at the table. To avoid God's judgment, you need to examine yourself. You need to treat the Lord's table seriously and be prepared to partake in a worthy manner.

The first step of examination is to ask yourself, *Am I in the faith?* Paul wrote to the Corinthians, "Test yourselves to see if you are in the faith. Examine yourselves. Or do you not recognize for yourselves that Jesus Christ is in you?—unless you fail the test" (2 Cor. 13:5). How would you know for sure whether you are in the faith? Paul said you would know by the Spirit of Jesus Christ, who is in you.

2. IN THE FOLLOWING SCRIPTURES UNDERLINE WAYS A PERSON CAN
   KNOW HE OR SHE IS IN THE FAITH. I'VE UNDERLINED ONE FOR YOU.
   - "The Spirit Himself testifies together with our spirit that we are
     God's children" (Rom. 8:16).
   - "This is how we are sure that we have come to know Him: by keep-
     ing His commands. The one who says, 'I have come to know Him,'
     without keeping His commands, is a liar, and the truth is not in
     him. But whoever keeps His word, truly in him the love of God is
     perfected. This is how we know we are in Him: the one who says
     he remains in Him should walk just as He walked" (1 John 2:3-6).
   - "The one who keeps His commands remains in Him, and He
     in him. And the way we know that He remains in us is from
     the Spirit He has given us" (1 John 3:24).
   - "This is how we know that we remain in Him and He in us:
     He has given to us from His Spirit" (1 John 4:13).

The Holy Spirit testifies or bears witness to your spirit that you belong to
God. The Holy Spirit's presence and work in you can help you know you
are God's child. John said you can know you are in Him if you obey Him.

3. DOES THE HOLY SPIRIT BEAR WITNESS TO YOU THAT YOU
   ARE A CHILD OF GOD? ☒ Yes ☐ No ☐ Not sure

4. DO YOU OBEY CHRIST AND WALK AS JESUS WALKED IN SUCH
   A WAY THAT YOU KNOW THE SPIRIT OF CHRIST DWELLS IN YOU?
   ☒ Yes ☐ No ☐ My inconsistency raises questions for me.

5. HAVE YOU PLACED YOUR FAITH AND TRUST IN JESUS CHRIST ALONE
   FOR YOUR SALVATION? ☒ Yes ☐ No

6. IF YOU HAVE A SAVING RELATIONSHIP WITH JESUS CHRIST, TAKE
   A MOMENT TO REFLECT ON THE OCCASION WHEN YOU ENTERED
   THAT RELATIONSHIP WITH HIM. NOTE SOME OF YOUR MEMORIES.
   *The Lord saved me during children's church.
   I was 7 yrs old and was very eager
   to tell my mom what had happened.*

Only those who have been genuinely converted by Jesus Christ and have entered a saving relationship with Him are worthy guests at the Lord's table. You are worthy because of what Christ has done in you, not because of your own righteousness or goodness.

If you have not yet turned to Jesus in saving faith, you should not participate in the Lord's table. If you have questions about your relationship with Jesus Christ, you have help: "The Spirit Himself testifies together with our spirit that we are God's children" (Rom. 8:16).

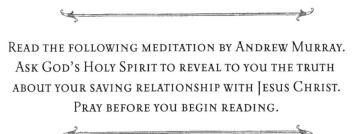

READ THE FOLLOWING MEDITATION BY ANDREW MURRAY.
ASK GOD'S HOLY SPIRIT TO REVEAL TO YOU THE TRUTH
ABOUT YOUR SAVING RELATIONSHIP WITH JESUS CHRIST.
PRAY BEFORE YOU BEGIN READING.

SELF-EXAMINATION

The problem of self-examination is simple. According to the apostle, there are but two conditions, either Jesus Christ is in you, or you are reprobate [rejected]: one of two. There is no third condition. The life of Christ in you may still be weak; but if you are truly born again and a child of God, Christ is in you. And then as a child you have access to the table of the Father and a share in the children's bread.

But if Christ is not in you, you are rejected. Nothing that is in you, nothing that you do, or are, or even desire and wish to be, makes you acceptable to God. The God against whom you have sinned inquires only about one thing: whether you have received His Son. "He that has the Son has the life" (AM). … If Christ is in you, you are acceptable to the Father. But if Christ is not in you, you are at the very same moment rejected. You have come in to the Lord's Supper without the wedding garment: your lot must be in the outermost darkness. You are unworthy. You eat judgment to yourself. You make yourself "guilty of the body and blood of the Lord" (AM).

Reader, how is it with you? What will God say of you when He sees you at the table? Will God look upon you as one of His children, who are very heartily welcome to Him at His table, or as an intruder who has no right to be at His table? Reader, What will

God say of you when He beholds you at His table? You are one of two things: you are either a true believer and a child of God, or you are not. If you are a child of God, you have a right to the table and to eat the bread of the Father, however feeble you may be. But if you are not a child of God—no true believer—you have no right to it. You may not go forward to it.

Examine your own self. Are you in the faith? Test yourself. Should it appear that you do not yet have Christ in you, then even today you can receive Him. There is still time. Without delay give yourself to Christ: in Him you have a right to the Lord's Table! (LT, pp. 32–35).

Next Andrew Murray offers two prayers. One is for all to pray, asking God to reveal the true condition of their hearts before Him. The other is for those who are not yet in the faith—those who realize Jesus does not yet live in them.

READ THE FIRST PRAYER AND LET IT BECOME YOUR PRAYER.
PRAY IT TO THE LORD.

PRAYER FOR ALL

"Search me, O God, and know my heart, try me and know my thoughts, and see if there is any wicked way in me and lead me in the way that is everlasting" (AM). Lord, You know how deceitful the heart is. It is deceitful far above all things. But, Lord, You know the heart, even my heart. Now I come to You, All-Knowing One. I set my heart before You with this prayer: Lord, make me know whether Jesus Christ is in me, or whether I am still without Him and rejected before You.

You, Yourself, saw to it that hypocrites should be cast out from the midst of Your people. You pointed out Achan. You made known Judas who dipped his hand in the dish with Your Son. … You are the King who scrutinized the guests and cast out the one without a wedding garment. … You are still mighty to search the hearts. Lord, hear now the prayer of Your people, and purge Your congregation. Let the life of the Spirit become so powerful that all doubts shall vanish. Help Your children to know and confess that Christ is in them. Let Your presence in our midst effect such a joy and such a reverence that those who merely confess Christ with their lips will be afraid. Permit the self-righteous to be revealed. Lord, make it known to many who are still content in uncertainty, whether Christ is in them or whether they are reprobate and rejected.

Great God, make this known to me: Is Jesus Christ in me? Let the Holy Spirit give me the blessed assurance of this. Then I will sit down with confidence as Your child at Your table.

And if Jesus Christ is still not in me, and I am still without Christ and rejected before You, make this known to me. Make me willing to know this. Give me a reverence so I'll not draw near to Your table except that Jesus Christ is in me. … Amen (LT, pp. 35–37).

7. As you have placed yourself before God seeking to know whether you are His child, what do you sense His Spirit has revealed to you? Check the statement that best describes your condition.

☒ a. Jesus is in me. I know it by the witness of His Spirit in me.
❑ b. My life in Christ is very weak, but Jesus is in me.
❑ c. I am still without Christ. He is not in me.
❑ d. I am still not sure which of these conditions is true of me.

If you checked a or b, skip to the closing activity of this lesson. If you are still unsure about your condition before God (d), keep reading and continue to seek His counsel. We have time. God wants you to know with certainty even more than you desire it, so continue to seek Him. If doubt persists, settle your relationship with Him in faith. If you realize you are still without Christ (c), move to the following prayer activity.

IF YOU CHECKED C OR D, READ THE FOLLOWING PRAYER
BY ANDREW MURRAY. IF YOU AGREE WITH THE PRAYER,
RECEIVE JESUS CHRIST AS YOUR SAVIOR.

PRAYER FOR ONE WITHOUT CHRIST

Lord God, I had thought of going forward to Your table. A sense of obligation came even to me, and I made myself ready for the hour of the feast. But, behold, Your word has made me afraid. It tells me that, if Jesus Christ is not in me, I am an unworthy guest.

Lord, have compassion upon me. I know that I may not sit down without the wedding garment. You are Lord of the table. Your word must prevail there. You are the Holy God. You cannot meet in love with the sinner who is not washed from his sin and clothed with the righteousness of Christ. Lord, I fear that I am still without that wedding garment: my sins are not forgiven. … Lord, have pity upon me. I dare not go to Your table. The bread of Your children is not for me.

I dare not go forward. And yet, Lord, I dare not remain away. To have no part in Jesus, no share in Your friendship, no place in the Marriage Supper of the Lamb on high—woe is me. Lord, have mercy upon me. Grant to me what I need for sitting down at Your table.

Lord God, I have heard of Your mercy. You give the wedding garment as a free gift. You forgive the worst sinner. Too long have I been content without really having Jesus Christ in me. Lord, now I come to You. I lay my unrighteousness before You. I am entirely under the power of sin, and cannot help myself. Lord, You alone can help me. Please receive me. I cast myself down here before You: I surrender myself to You. This day let the blood of Jesus wash me and make me clean.

Lord Jesus, given by the Father for me, I receive You. I receive You, Lord, as my Savior. I believe that You are for me. Here I give You my heart—my poor, sinful heart. Come and dwell in it, and let me also know that Jesus Christ is in me.

My God, my soul cries out and longs for You: make me truly a partaker of Jesus Christ. Amen (LT, pp. 37–39).

8. IF YOU HAVE JUST PRAYED TO RECEIVE CHRIST, CONTACT YOUR PASTOR TO SHARE THE GOOD NEWS. WHOM ELSE DO YOU NEED TO TELL? WRITE NOTES ON "MY PREPARATIONS" LIST ON PAGE 127.

Wednesday

Day 10 ~ Judge Yourself

> *"If we were properly evaluating ourselves,*
> *we would not be judged, but when we are judged,*
> *we are <u>disciplined by the Lord</u>, so that*
> *<u>we may not be condemned with the world</u>."*

1 Corinthians 11:31-32

*T*oday we will continue to prepare ourselves to be worthy guests at the Lord's table. Not only do you need to examine yourself to learn whether you are in the faith, but you also need to examine yourself to determine whether you are clean from sin. God gives you a choice. You can either judge yourself and thoroughly repent of your sin, or you can hold on to your sin and come under God's judgment and discipline.

‣ 1. READ WHAT PAUL WROTE TO THE CORINTHIANS. CIRCLE THE WORDS *judged* AND *judgment*. THEN ANSWER THE QUESTIONS THAT FOLLOW.

"Whoever eats the bread or drinks the cup of the Lord in an unworthy way will be guilty of sin against the body and blood of the Lord. So a man should examine himself; in this way he should eat of the bread and drink of the cup. For whoever eats and drinks without recognizing the body, eats and drinks judgment on himself. This is why many are sick and ill among you, and many have fallen asleep. If we were properly evaluating ourselves, we would not be judged.

but when we are ~~judged,~~ we are ~~disciplined by the Lord, so that we~~ ~~may not be condemned with the world~~" (1 Cor. 11:27-32).

2. IF YOU JUDGE YOURSELF, WHAT WILL YOU AVOID? *judgement from the Lord*

3. WHY DOES GOD JUDGE OR DISCIPLINE HIS PEOPLE? *So that we may not be condemned w/ the world. (Judgement is different from condemnation.)*

4. USING THE PASSAGE ABOVE, FILL IN THE BLANKS TO DESCRIBE WAYS GOD MAY DISCIPLINE CHRISTIANS FOR NOT TAKING SERIOUSLY THE BODY OF THE LORD.

"That is why many among you are *weak* and *sickly*, and a number of you have *fallen* *asleep*."

If you judge yourself, you will not come under God's judgment. When God judges or disciplines you, He does it so that you will not be condemned with the world. Some of the Corinthians had experienced God's discipline in physical ways: they were weak or sick or had fallen asleep (died). This teaching is why churches have historically taken the Lord's table ~~very seriously~~.

5. BASED ON THIS TRUTH, WHICH OF THE FOLLOWING WOULD YOU RATHER DO? CHECK ONE.
   ☒ a. I would rather judge myself, repent of sin, and be right with God.
   ❏ b. I would rather hold on to my sinful ways and ignore or casually treat the fact that Christ's body was broken for me. I'll take my chances of being disciplined by God.

I assume you chose a. The second choice would indicate that you do not have a ~~healthy reverence for Holy God~~.

❧ 6. READ WHAT GOD SAYS ABOUT THE WAY WE DEAL WITH OUR SINS.
   THEN ANSWER THE QUESTIONS THAT FOLLOW.
   "He who conceals his sins does not prosper,
      but whoever confesses and renounces them finds mercy.
   Blessed is the man who always fears the LORD,
      but he who hardens his heart falls into trouble"
   (Prov. 28:13-14, NIV).

❧ 7. WHAT DOES A PERSON FIND WHEN HE CONFESSES AND RENOUNCES
   PERSONAL SIN?
   _____ *mercy* _____

❧ 8. WHAT HAPPENS TO A PERSON WHO HARDENS HIS HEART TOWARD
   GOD AND HIDES OR CONCEALS HIS SIN?

   _____ *he does not prosper* _____

❧ 9. WHAT IS THE CONDITION OF A PERSON "WHO ALWAYS FEARS
   THE LORD" (V. 14, NIV)?
   _____ *Blessed* _____

When you confess and renounce (quit) your sin, you find mercy from God.
He forgives and cleanses you from sin. You do this because you have a
healthy fear and reverence for your holy God. The person who covers and
tries to hide his sin will not prosper. In fact, he or she "falls into trouble"
(v. 14, NIV). You cannot hide your sin from God. He loves you too much
to leave you in an unworthy life and in the gutter with sin. Because of His
love for you, He will discipline you (see Heb. 12:5-6). God disciplines you
because He loves you too much to let you continue living with less than
the abundant life Jesus died to give you.

❧ 10. READ THE FOLLOWING SCRIPTURES, WHICH TELL HOW WE SHOULD
   DEAL WITH SIN. ONE OR MORE STATEMENTS FOLLOW EACH SCRIP-
   TURE. CIRCLE EACH STATEMENT *T* (TRUE) OR *F* (FALSE).
   "This, then, is the judgment: the light has come into the world, and
   people loved darkness rather than the light because their deeds
   were evil. For everyone who practices wicked things hates the light

and avoids it, so that his deeds may not be exposed. But anyone who lives by the truth comes to the light, so that his works may be shown to be accomplished by God" (John 3:19-21).

11. T (F) CHRISTIANS SHOULD TRY TO COVER UP THEIR SIN AS IF NOTHING WERE WRONG.

12. (T) F PEOPLE WHO DO EVIL TEND TO HIDE FROM GOD'S LIGHT SO THAT THEIR EVIL DEEDS WILL NOT BE EXPOSED.

"I preached that they should repent and turn to God and prove their repentance by their deeds" (Acts 26:20, NIV).

13. T (F) I PROVE MY REPENTANCE BY WHAT I SAY, NOT WHAT I DO.

"God's solid foundation stands firm, having this inscription: 'The Lord knows those who are His,' and Everyone who names the name of the Lord must turn away from unrighteousness" (2 Tim. 2:19).

14. T (F.) I CAN TRUTHFULLY CLAIM THAT JESUS IS MY LORD AND LIVE A WICKED LIFE AT THE SAME TIME.

"If we walk in the light as He Himself is in the light, we have fellowship with one another, and the blood of Jesus His Son cleanses us from all sin. If we say, 'We have no sin,' we are deceiving ourselves, and the truth is not in us. If we confess our sins, He is faithful and righteous to forgive us our sins and to cleanse us from all unrighteousness. If we say, 'We have not sinned,' we make Him a liar, and His word is not in us" (1 John 1:7-10).

15. (T) F IF I CONFESS MY SIN, GOD WILL FORGIVE AND PURIFY ME.

(Answers: 11-F, 12-T, 13-F, 14-F, 15-T)

If you live by God's truth, you will voluntarily come into the light and get rid of your sin. Trying to hide your sin indicates that Jesus is not really your Lord as you claim. You need to confess (agree with God about) your sin and turn away from wickedness. When you do, God forgives, cleanses, and restores you to right fellowship with Himself. I encourage you to judge yourself before coming to the Lord's table. The Holy Spirit, who lives in you, has the job assignment of convicting you of sin. He will assist you in examining your life to discover any sin you need to confess and renounce.

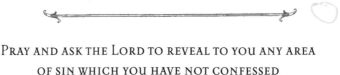

PRAY AND ASK THE LORD TO REVEAL TO YOU ANY AREA
OF SIN WHICH YOU HAVE NOT CONFESSED
AND FROM WHICH YOU HAVE NOT TURNED AWAY.

16. PRAYERFULLY READ THE FOLLOWING LIST OF SINS AND AREAS OF SIN.
ASK THE LORD TO REVEAL TO YOU ANY AREA IN WHICH YOU HAVE
NOT TURNED AWAY FROM SIN AND EXPERIENCED HIS CLEANSING.
ASK HIM TO SHOW YOU ANY SIN THAT HINDERS YOUR FELLOWSHIP
WITH HIM. YOU MAY WANT TO CHECK ANY GOD IDENTIFIES SO THAT
YOU CAN SERIOUSLY DEAL WITH YOUR SIN. YOU MAY PREFER TO
WRITE THESE ON A SEPARATE SHEET OF PAPER THAT CAN BE DISPOSED
OF LATER.

- ❑ Unbelief—not believing God will keep His word
- ❑ Rebellion—disobedience, not letting Christ be Lord of all, living my own way
- ❑ Pride/arrogance—thinking more highly of myself than I ought, more than what God knows to be true of me
- ❑ Bitterness, unforgiveness, holding a grudge
- ❑ Sins of the tongue—gossip, slander, murmuring, lying, cursing, filthy speech, vain talk, obscenity
- ❑ Dishonesty, deceit
- ❑ Mental impurity, filthy thought life
- ❑ Addiction to harmful or illegal substances
- ❑ Addiction to pornography (either visual or written)
- ❑ Sexual immorality
- ❑ Stealing, cheating, embezzlement
- ❑ Anger, hatred, malice, rage, uncontrolled temper
- ❑ Idolatry—worshiping another god or loving something or someone more than I love God
- ☒ Poor stewardship of my time and resources

❑ Taking unfair advantage of others, oppressing others
❑ Prayerlessness
❑ Disobedience to the Lord's clear commands
❑ Injustice, failing to defend the oppressed
❑ Murder, hating others without a cause
❑ Causing strife, conflict, and dissension in the church
❑ Worshiping with my lips when my heart is far away from loving the Lord
❑ Leaving my first love for Christ by loving other people, things, or activities more than the Lord
❑ Others: _____

This is certainly not a complete list of sins. You can miss God's standards in many ways through your thoughts, actions, and words. <u>Develop a heart that is ready to confess and repent at the slightest whisper of conviction from the Holy Spirit</u>. If God has convicted you of sin, take these actions now to get right with Him.

1. Confess: agree with God that you have sinned.
2. Repent: turn away from your sin and turn to God to live His way.
3. Seek the Lord's forgiveness and cleansing.
4. Show your repentance by a changed life/deeds.

Here's what God does with your sin when you confess and repent:

> *"It is I who <u>sweep away</u> your transgressions …*
> *and <u>remember your sins no more</u>" (Isa. 43:25).*

> *"He will … <u>cast all our sins</u>*
> *<u>into the depths of the sea</u>" (Mic. 7:19).*

Talk to the Lord about any sin He has revealed. Judge yourself. Confess your sin and repent. Thank Him for His forgiveness and cleansing. Commit to live His way and for His glory. If you know actions you need to take, write them on "My Preparations" list on page 127.

Day 11 ~ Watch and Pray

"Stay awake and pray,
so that you won't enter into temptation.
The spirit is willing, but the flesh is weak."

Matthew 26:41

Yesterday you may have become painfully aware of areas of weakness in your life—temptations to sin where you are too weak to resist. I have good news. You do not have to live as a slave to sin. Paul wrote, "Thank God that, although you used to be slaves of sin, you obeyed from the heart that pattern of teaching you were entrusted to, and having been liberated from sin, you became enslaved to righteousness" (Rom. 6:17-18). Because of Christ, you can be set free from sin.

1. READ OR SING "JESUS PAID IT ALL" ON PAGE 53. WHAT DOES THE WRITER SAY WE OWE JESUS? UNDERLINE IT.

Jesus gave His all for us. We owe our all to Him. Paul said it this way: "I ... urge you to walk worthy of the calling you have received" (Eph. 4:1). We cannot be strong enough in ourselves to live such a life. Jesus has a way for you to be strong against temptation. Following the last supper, Jesus delivered a warning to Peter.

Jesus Paid It All

Elvina M. Hall

I hear the Savior say,
"Thy strength indeed is small,
Child of weakness, watch and pray,
Find in Me thine all in all."

Lord, now indeed I find
Thy pow'r, and Thine alone,
Can change the leper's spots
And melt the heart of stone.

For nothing good have I
Whereby Thy grace to claim;

I'll wash my garments white
In the blood of Calv'ry's Lamb.

And when, before the throne,
I stand in Him complete,
"Jesus died my soul to save,"
My lips shall still repeat.

Refrain
Jesus paid it all,
All to Him I owe;
Sin had left a crimson stain,
He washed it white as snow.

---

2. AS YOU READ THIS SCRIPTURE, UNDERLINE THE WARNINGS.

"Simon, Simon, look out! Satan has asked to sift you like wheat. But I have prayed for you that your faith may not fail. And you, when you have turned back, strengthen your brothers."

"Lord," he told Him, "I'm ready to go with You both to prison and to death!"

"I tell you, Peter," He said, "the rooster will not crow today until you deny three times that you know Me!" (Luke 22:31-34).

Jesus warned Peter that Satan was about to test his faith. When Peter affirmed his willingness to die with Jesus, Jesus explained that he would deny Him three times that very night. Then Jesus took His disciples across the valley to the Garden of Gethsemane. To eight of the disciples Jesus said, "Sit here while I go over there and pray" (Matt. 26:36). But He took Peter, James, and John deeper into the garden and asked them to watch and pray. When He returned, He found them sleeping.

3. UNDERLINE THE REASON JESUS ASKED PETER TO PRAY.

"He came to the disciples and found them sleeping. He asked Peter, 'So, couldn't you stay awake with Me one hour?' <u>Stay awake and pray, so that you won't enter into temptation.</u> The spirit is willing, but the flesh is weak'" (Matt. 26:37-41).

Jesus asked Peter to watch and pray so that he would not fall into temptation. Instead of praying, Peter yielded to the weakness of his body and slept. Jesus addressed this message to Peter, knowing Peter would not be prepared for the testing he was about to face because he had not spent time in prayer. Because Peter allowed his body (flesh) to win over his spirit, he failed in his time of testing and denied the Lord. Later he went out and bitterly wept because of his sin. This is an example of why we must be people of prayer. Prayer is the way we gain God's strength through the Holy Spirit to resist temptation to sin.

4. THINK ABOUT THE CONNECTION BETWEEN THE AMOUNT OF TIME YOU PRAY AND YOUR ABILITY TO RESIST THE TEMPTATION TO SIN. WHICH OF THE FOLLOWING IS MOST TRUE OF YOU? CHECK ONE OR WRITE YOUR OWN.

❑ a. I have found that because of my prayer times with Christ,
☒ I have strength to resist much temptation to sin that comes my way.

❑ b. I don't have much strength to resist temptation to sin. I realize I'm like Peter. I am weak because of little prayer.

❑ c. I spend much time in prayer, and yet I still seem to be weak when temptation comes. I don't understand why.

❑ d. Other: _____

_____

GET ALONE WITH JESUS IN PRAYER. PRAY NOW, BUT IF TIME IS SHORT, CARVE OUT A LARGER BLOCK OF TIME SOON. WATCH AND PRAY SO THAT YOU WILL NOT YIELD TO TEMPTATION.

Day 12 ~ Remove Idols of the Heart

"If your heart turns away and you
do not listen and you are led astray
to bow down to other gods and worship them,
I tell you today that you will certainly perish."

Deuteronomy 30:17-18

God spoke to Ezekiel about the elders in Israel: "These men have <u>set up idols in their hearts</u> and have put <u>sinful stumbling blocks before their faces</u>" (Ezek. 14:3). Jesus said the first and greatest commandment is this: "Love the Lord your God with all your heart, with all your soul, and with all your mind" (Matt. 22:37). Anything that takes the place of your first love for God can be a false god or an idol of the heart. Leaving your first love for God by turning to an idol of the heart can be a serious matter.

is

1. READ REVELATION 2:4-5 BELOW. UNDERLINE THE PHRASE THAT DESCRIBES WHAT JESUS SAID HE WOULD DO TO THE CHURCH OF EPHESUS IF THE CHURCH DID NOT REPENT AND RETURN TO ITS FIRST LOVE FOR HIM.

"I have this against you: you have abandoned the love you had at first. Remember then how far you have fallen; repent, and do the works you did at first. Otherwise, I will come to you and <u>remove your lamp-stand [church] from its place</u>—unless you repent" (Rev. 2:4-5).

Jesus said He would remove the church from its place if it did not return to its first love for Him. Violating the first and greatest commandment is serious with God. <u>An idol of the heart is anything that captures your love and attention in a way that keeps you from your first love for Him.</u>

2. IN EACH OF THE FOLLOWING SCRIPTURES, CIRCLE THE WORD OR PHRASE THAT DESCRIBES SOMETHING THAT CAN GET IN THE WAY OF YOUR FIRST LOVE FOR GOD OR THAT CAN BE AN IDOL OF THE HEART.
  - "No one can be a slave of two masters, since either he will hate one and love the other, or be devoted to one and despise the other. You cannot be slaves of God and of <u>money</u>" (Matt. 6:24).
  - "Do not love the <u>world</u> or the <u>things that belong to the world</u>. If anyone loves the world, love for the Father is not in him" (1 John 2:15).

Can you imagine how dangerous this matter is for many Christians and churches today? Love of money, the world, or anything in the world prevents you from fully loving God. The materialism of many Christians is a major idol of the heart they may not even recognize. How about you?

3. IF YOU WERE HONEST BEFORE GOD, HOW WOULD YOU RATE YOUR LOVE OF MONEY AND THINGS? CHECK THE RESPONSE THAT IS MOST LIKE YOU OR WRITE YOUR OWN.
  - ❑ a. I'm obsessed with the love of money and things. Much of my life revolves around seeking money or buying and enjoying things that are beyond basic necessities.
  - ❑ b. I probably love things too much. If I had to choose between my things and fully loving the Lord, I might be tempted to waver.
  - ❑ c. I don't have much in the way of material things, but I'd have to confess my desire for those things is far too strong.
  - ❑ d. Though I seek to have a first love for the Lord, sometimes I realize my things are too important to me.
  - ☒ e. On several occasions God has led me to choose Him over money and things, and I'm growing more and more fully in love with Him.
  - ❑ f. Other: _____

IF YOU REALIZE YOU MAY HAVE IDOLS IN YOUR HEART,
CONFESS YOUR SIN TO THE LORD. ASK HIM TO HELP YOU
IDENTIFY THE IDOLS. ASK HIM TO HELP YOU
RETURN TO YOUR FIRST LOVE FOR HIM.

Jacob's Family Assembly

Jacob returned to the promised land after being away for years building a family. Fearing the people of the land, he said, "We are few in number; and if they unite against me and attack me, I and my household will be destroyed" (Gen. 34:30). When Jacob was in distress, God told him to return to Bethel for a time of worship. Bethel is where God had met him years before when Jacob was running away from his brother, Esau. There God had entered the covenant with Jacob that He had established with Abraham and Isaac before him. Now God was preparing to renew His covenant promises with Jacob and his sons. Jacob knew his family needed to get ready to meet with Holy God.

4. AS YOU READ THE DESCRIPTION OF THIS FAMILY'S SACRED ASSEMBLY, LOOK FOR THE THINGS JACOB'S FAMILY DID TO GET READY TO MEET WITH GOD AT BETHEL.

"Jacob said to his family and all who were with him, 'Get rid of the foreign gods that are among you. Purify yourselves and change your clothes. We must get up and go to Bethel. I will build an altar there to the God who answered me in my day of distress. He has been with me everywhere I have gone.' Then they gave Jacob all their foreign gods and their earrings, and Jacob hid them under the oak near Shechem. When they set out, a terror from God came over the cities around them, and they did not pursue Jacob's sons" (Gen. 35:2-5).

5. WHAT DID JACOB'S FAMILY DO TO PREPARE TO MEET WITH GOD?

_____

Jacob consecrated his family members by having them put away their foreign gods and the impurities they had accumulated. They even changed clothes to be physically clean before the Lord. God responded by causing the people of the land to fear God and stay away from Jacob and his family. Then at Bethel Jacob's family had a wonderful worship experience. God renewed His covenant with Jacob and gave him a new name—Israel (see Gen. 35:6-15).

As you look forward to meeting with God at the Lord's table, you need to examine your heart, your relationships, your activities, and your household possessions to learn whether you have any false gods or idols of the heart you need to deal with. Idols can be things, relationships, or activities. They may not be evil in themselves, but perhaps they have captured too much of your love. Examples could include—

+ hobbies or collections;
+ a material object you treasure too dearly;
+ material things that consume far too much of your time using them or maintaining them;
+ things that you own to impress others or that cause you to feel arrogant or condescending toward others;
+ things you have purchased for yourself that you know God didn't want you to have;
+ activities you love that consume too much of your time and may keep you from your time with God or from obediently serving Him (like television, sports, work/career, or recreation);
+ relationships that keep you from your first love for Christ.

One way to test something is to ask yourself, *If God asked me to give this up, would I resist Him or struggle to obey?* If you are holding on too tightly, the item may be an idol of the heart. Only the Lord can reveal to you whether something has captured your love, but He will if you ask Him.

<hr>

ASK THE LORD TO GIVE YOU DISCERNMENT ABOUT THIS MATTER
OF HEART IDOLS. IF YOU AREN'T SURE WHETHER AN ITEM,
A RELATIONSHIP, OR AN ACTIVITY IS AN IDOL, TALK TO THE
LORD ABOUT IT UNTIL YOU HAVE PEACE ABOUT HIS ASSESSMENT.

6. ON A SEPARATE SHEET OF PAPER, LIST THINGS, RELATIONSHIPS, OR ACTIVITIES GOD BRINGS TO MIND AS POSSIBLE IDOLS OF YOUR HEART.

I used to collect arrowheads. I treasured them. At one point I realized they had become idols of my heart. I came to the conviction I had to get rid of them to break the hold they had on me. The owner of a rock shop expressed interest in buying the arrowheads. I made the long trip to his shop ready to sell my entire collection. When he looked at them, he decided they were not the quality he wanted. He said he did not care to buy them. I was disappointed as I drove back home.

Then I remembered God's dealing with Abraham and his son Isaac. Once Abraham proved his willingness to obey God and offer Isaac as a sacrifice, God gave Isaac back to his father (see Gen. 22:1-18). Once I had given my arrowheads to the Lord by agreeing to sell them, their hold on my heart was broken. Later I sold some of my best ones just to make sure their hold on me was gone. Then I gave the money to a Christian ministry to make sure my motives were pure.

If you realize you have a heart idol, you may need to throw it away, destroy it, give it away, sell it, or do something else to break its hold on your heart. You may even need to evaluate your use of television, the Internet, or another activity to determine whether these are heart idols. God may guide you to exercise temperance in these activities. In other cases He may ask you to quit the activity altogether. Remember that returning to your first love for Christ is serious business.

IF YOU HAVE IDENTIFIED IDOLS OF YOUR HEART, PRAY THROUGH THE FOLLOWING STEPS AND CHECK EACH ONE WHEN YOU FINISH.

❑ Confess to the Lord that you have given your love and attention to these items. Agree with Him that you have sinned.
❑ Ask Him to forgive and cleanse you.
❑ Ask Him to set you free from your love for these things. Remember the height from which you have fallen. Return to your first love.
❑ Pledge to Him your love and desire to please and obey Him.

Day 13 ~ Consecrate Your Home

> *"The LORD said to Moses,*
> *'Go to the people and consecrate them.'"*
>
> Exodus 19:10, NIV

As you prepare to meet with God at the Lord's table, consecrate yourself, your family, and your home. This is a time for a family sacred assembly (like Jacob's). If you live alone or your family doesn't know the Lord, use today's instructions in the way that will be most appropriate for you.

1. PREPARE FOR A FAMILY ASSEMBLY. BEFORE THE TIME FOR THE LORD'S TABLE, MAKE PLANS FOR A FAMILY GATHERING. YOU MAY NEED TO ADJUST YOUR SCHEDULE TO ANOTHER NIGHT OR TIME SO THAT EVERYONE CAN BE PRESENT. WHEN WILL YOU MEET AND WITH WHOM?

_____

This lesson will prepare you to consecrate your home. Use the following material to guide an experience with the family members you have listed.

2. STUDY THE FOLLOWING ILLUSTRATIONS FROM THE BIBLE AND BE PREPARED TO READ THEM OR TELL THEM IN YOUR OWN WORDS.

Moses Consecrated the People

When Israel had left Egypt, the people came to the mountain of God, where Moses would be given the Ten Commandments. Prior to meeting with the people, the Lord announced His plans and gave Moses these instructions: "'Go to the people and purify them today and tomorrow. They must wash their clothes and be prepared by the third day, for on the third day the LORD will come down on Mount Sinai in the sight of all the people.' ... Then Moses came down from the mountain to the people and consecrated them, and they washed their clothes. He said to the people, 'Be prepared by the third day. Do not have sexual relations with women.' On the third day, when morning came, there was thunder and lightning, a thick cloud on the mountain, and a loud trumpet sound, so that all the people in the camp shuddered. Then Moses brought the people out of the camp to meet God" (Ex. 19:10-17).

God is still a holy God; yet we are far too casual when we enter His presence. We may have allowed many impurities of the world into our homes and lives without considering whether they are acceptable to the Lord. Or we may have failed to get rid of evil things from our old, sinful lives after we came to faith in Christ.

A Bonfire at Ephesus

When Paul began a church in Ephesus, God demonstrated His power by working miracles through him. On one occasion great "fear fell on all of them, and the name of the Lord Jesus was magnified. And many who had become believers came confessing and disclosing their practices, while many of those who had practiced magic collected their books and burned them in front of everyone. So they calculated their value, and found it to be 50,000 pieces of silver. In this way the Lord's message flourished and prevailed" (Acts 19:17-20).

🔖 3. WHAT TWO THINGS DID THE EPHESIAN CHRISTIANS DO?

    a. They openly confessed their _their occultic practices_

    b. They burned their _occultic books_ .

When the people realized how holy God really is, they got rid of the unholy things in their lives, even when the action was costly. They openly confessed and turned away from their evil deeds, burning the things related to their former practice of sorcery. The result was that the work of the kingdom spread and grew in power.

Stop and pray, asking God to reveal to you and your family members things in your home that represent the impurities of the world He would like for you to get rid of. Confess to the Lord that you want to be clean and pure before Him. Give Him permission to clean your home of impurities. Check here after you have prayed: ☒

Begin a process of consecrating your home. You may want to conduct a family tour of your house room by room. Imagine Jesus is coming to your home to take a careful look in every room. He will see the things in your closets and drawers. He will see the music you listen to and the videotapes or DVDs you watch. He will look on your bookshelves. Nothing will escape His pure gaze. Ask yourselves, *What is in our home that we would be ashamed for Jesus to see?* These are the things you need to throw away.

4. Invite family members to clean the house of spiritual and moral impurities that may have accumulated. read this list and then walk through each room, cleaning as you go. In every case let God's Holy Spirit guide your consciences. If you have doubts or disagreement about an item, pause and pray about it, asking the Lord how He thinks about it.

- Music CDs, audiotapes, or records with lyrics that are impure, ungodly, or unholy
- Movies, DVDs, or videotapes that have language, images, themes, or actions that are impure or unholy, especially those that are sources of temptation toward lust, sensuality, violence, or materialism (Don't let the world's rating system determine your criteria for acceptable content. What is pleasing and acceptable to the Lord?)
- Books used for false worship or that encourage ungodly behavior

- Novels, magazines, or other printed literature that is visually or mentally pornographic
- Books, clothing, or items used by secret organizations that are incompatible with serving and worshiping God alone
- Images, souvenirs, pictures, sculptures, and paintings that may be items of worship in false religions or are used to practice witchcraft or the occult (for example, a Ouija Board or a statue of a false god)
- Alcohol, drugs, tobacco, or another substance that has become a vice to you, that can damage your body, or that contributes to intemperance
- Games or computer programs that have impure, wicked, ungodly, or unholy subject matter or practices; games that lead to impure physical contact or interaction between the sexes
- Clothing you know is immodest or is intended to be seductive
- Any other material thing that is a source of temptation to sin

---

AFTER YOU HAVE COLLECTED THE THINGS THAT NEED TO BE DISPOSED OF, CHECK THE FOLLOWING STEPS AS YOU RESPOND TO GOD IN PRAYER.

❏ Confess to the Lord that you have tolerated evils and impurities that are not appropriate for His holy people. Agree with Him that you have sinned.
❏ Ask Him to forgive and cleanse you.
❏ Ask Him to set you free from any desire to hold on to the impurities. Ask Him to change your heart in love and obedience to Him.
☒ Pledge to Him your renewed loyalty, love, and desire to please Him and obey Him.
☒ Thank Him for the purity and godly character He is bringing into your lives.

---

5. NOW DISPOSE OF THE ITEMS THAT NEED TO BE THROWN OUT. DO NOT SELL OR GIVE AWAY THINGS THAT ARE EVIL, UNHOLY, OR IMPURE. MAKE SURE THE ITEMS ARE DISPOSED OF PERMANENTLY SO THAT OTHERS WILL NOT BE POLLUTED BY THEM.

Sunday

Day 14 ~ Group Session 2

OPEN WITH PRAYER

Thank God for providing forgiveness and cleansing for sin. Thank Him that you can be set free from the power of sin. Ask Him to be a refiner's fire and to remove impurities in your lives and in your church.

SING/LISTEN

Select a song or hymn that focuses your attention on Christ and His sacrifice on the cross. Sing it together, read the lyrics, or listen to someone sing it live or from a recording.

REVIEW DAYS 8–13

1. What Scripture, statement, idea, testimony, or illustration that you read this week was most significant or meaningful to you and why?
2. What are seven things Jesus accomplished through His blood? (See p. 35.)
3. What are some possible consequences of partaking of the Lord's table in an unworthy manner? (See 1 Cor. 11:27-32.)
4. How can a person know that he or she is in the faith? (See activity 2, p. 41.)
5. What is the value of judging ourselves rather than waiting for God to do so? (See day 10, p. 46.)
6. How should a Christian deal with sin in his or her life?
7. What is the connection between prayer and the ability to resist temptation?
8. What are some common idols of the heart that people may worship today? If God identified any of these in your life, how have you responded to Him?

9. What are some ways you (and/or your family) found that you have allowed moral or spiritual impurities to enter your home? How did you deal with them? (See day 13, p. 60.)

RESPOND TO LEARNING ACTIVITIES
1. Day 8 , activity 3 (p. 37). What emotions did you have as you drew blood on the picture of Christ?
2. Day 8, activity 4 (p. 38). How did you describe your love for Jesus?
3. Day 9, activity 6 (p. 41). Share memories of the day you first entered a faith relationship with Jesus Christ.
4. Day 9, activity 8 (p. 45). If anyone prayed to receive Christ this week, tell us your story.

PRAY TOGETHER
Divide into small groups (three to five) of the same gender for this prayer time. Pray together and for one another.
1. Spend time thanking Jesus for His sacrifice for your sins.
2. Confess to Him your desire to live worthy lives, as well as your dependence on Him for help to do so.
3. "Confess your sins to one another and pray for one another, so that you may be healed" (Jas. 5:16). Share general areas of past weakness or sin and present areas of temptation (for example, honesty, clean language, pure thought life, moral purity, forgiveness, obedience, faithful stewardship). Describe idols of the heart or impurities that need to be put away. Pray for one another about specific areas of need. You might ask one another, How may we pray for your spiritual victory over sin? After a person shares a request, take time to pray for him or her before hearing from the next person. Take time to pray for each one in your group.
4. Pray that your church and its leaders (both paid and volunteer) will be pure, holy, godly, and victorious over sin.
5. Pray that specific church members, groups, and families will be strong and victorious over sin.

PREVIEW THE COMING WEEK

⊰ Day 15 ~ Reconcile with Those You've Offended ⊱

"If you are offering your gift on the altar, and there you remember that your brother has something against you, leave your gift there in front of the altar. First go and be reconciled with your brother, and then come and offer your gift."

Matthew 5:23-24

When Paul wrote to the Corinthians about the Lord's Supper, he expressed his concerns about the divisions in the church: "I hear that when you come together as a church there are divisions among you. ... When you come together in one place, it is not really to eat the Lord's Supper. For in eating, each one takes his own supper ahead of others, and one person is hungry while another is drunk! ... Do you look down on the church of God and embarrass those who have nothing? What should I say to you? Should I praise you? I do not praise you for this!" (1 Cor. 11:18-22).

The church often had a meal in addition to the elements of the Lord's Supper itself. The rich neglected the poor and showed contempt for the body of Christ. Paul wrote other statements to the Corinthians about divisions in their church: "I urge you, brothers, in the name of our Lord Jesus Christ, that you all say the same thing, that there be no divisions among you, and that you be united with the same understanding and the same conviction" (1 Cor. 1:10). "Brothers, I was not able to speak to you as spiritual people but as people of the flesh. ... For since there is envy and strife among you, are you not fleshly and living like ordinary people?" (1 Cor. 3:1-3).

❧ 1. When jealousy, quarreling, or division is in your church, what are the members acting like?

_____

Disunity in Christ's body is a serious sin. Churches that are divided and quarreling look like the world, not like followers of Christ. The night before Jesus went to the cross, He prayed for our unity: "I am in them and You are in Me. May they be made completely one, so the world may know You have sent Me and have loved them as You have loved Me" (John 17:23).

Christian unity is the most convincing evidence to the lost world that Jesus is the Savior sent from God. That also means our disunity is probably the greatest hindrance to leading others to faith in Christ. If you have broken relationships with brothers and sisters in Christ, you must be reconciled.

❧ 2. Read the following statements Jesus made about the importance of right relationships between believers. Underline what a person needs to do to get the relationship right.

 • "If you are offering your gift on the altar, and there you remember that your brother has something against you, leave your gift there in front of the altar. First go and be reconciled with your brother, and then come and offer your gift" (Matt. 5:23-24).
 • "Whenever you stand praying, if you have anything against anyone, forgive him, so that your Father in heaven will also forgive you your wrongdoing" (Mark 11:25).

❧ 3. Match the conditions described in 1 and 2 below with the correct responses that follow them (a, b, c, or d).
 _d_ 1. If I am the offender and my brother holds a grudge against me,
 _c_ 2. If my brother has offended me and I am holding a grudge,
 a. I should ignore the problem and hope it goes away.
 b. I should wait until my brother takes the first step by coming to me to get things right.
 c. I should immediately forgive the offense even if my brother has not asked for forgiveness.
 d. I should delay my worship and first reconcile with my brother so that my worship will be acceptable.

Jesus knows the importance of right relationships in the body of Christ. He commands us to respond in a way that is <u>directly opposite to what our human nature would suggest</u>. If I am the offender, my worship isn't acceptable until I've been reconciled. If my brother is the offender, I should forgive him even though he may not have asked for forgiveness. That's pretty radical, isn't it? But that's why unity can be such a powerful testimony to a watching world. The rest of the world doesn't act that way. (Answers: 1-d, 2-c)

4. IN THE FOLLOWING LIST CHECK ANY RELATIONSHIP IN YOUR LIFE THAT NEEDS RECONCILIATION. IF YOU WISH, WRITE A NAME OR INITIALS IN THE MARGIN AS A REMINDER OF A RELATIONSHIP THAT NEEDS TO BE MADE RIGHT.

☒ Have I mistreated anyone by my actions or words? *All my kids*

❏ Have I stolen from a person, an organization, a business, my employer, or anyone else?

❏ Do I hold a grudge or bitterness in my heart toward anyone?

❏ Have I gossiped about or slandered another person?

❏ Have I borrowed anything I have failed to return?

❏ Has God impressed me to do something to meet another person's needs, and I have failed to obey Him?

❏ Have I done anything illegal I need to confess?

❏ Have I lied to anyone or falsified information?

❏ Have I hurt someone because of an immoral act and covered it up?

❏ Am I currently in a wrong or immoral relationship with anyone?

❏ Have I been guilty of not expressing gratitude to a person or group when I should have? Am I taking someone for granted and need to show my gratitude in words and deeds?

❏ Have I allowed jealousy, envy, or resentment to have a negative effect on the way I have related to a person or group?

❏ Have I allowed pride to keep me from relating to a person who needed a friend?

❏ Have I sinned against God and another person or group by committing any of the following sins?

❏ Anger	☒ Anxiety	❏ Arguing
❏ Arrogance	❏ Bitterness	❏ Blasphemy
☒ Boasting	❏ Coarse talking	❏ Conceit
❏ Complaining	❏ Competition	❏ Covetousness

❑ Cursing   ❑ Critical spirit   ❑ Deception
❑ Controlling spirit ❑ Discord   ☒ Disorder
❑ Divisiveness   ❑ Envy   ❑ Factions
❑ Faultfinding   ❑ Fear   ❑ Fits of rage
❑ Gossip   ❑ Greed   ❑ Grumbling
❑ Hatred   ❑ Hypocrisy   ❑ Impatience
❑ Impurity   ❑ Independence   ❑ Injustice
☒ Insensitivity   ❑ Jealousy   ❑ Lack of love
❑ Lies   ❑ Malice   ❑ Oppression
❑ Persecution   ❑ Prejudice   ❑ Pride
❑ Quarreling   ❑ Resentment   ❑ Revenge
❑ Rudeness   ❑ Slander   ❑ Strife
❑ Unbelief   ❑ Self-seeking
❑ Judgmental spirit ❑ Intolerance of differences
❑ Unforgiveness   ❑ Lawsuits among believers
❑ Spirit of superiority ❑ Keeping a record of wrongs
❑ Selfish ambition   ❑ Provoking one another
❑ Self-righteousness ❑ Struggle for control
                     ❑ Delighting in a brother's downfall

If the Holy Spirit has brought to your mind any relationships that are broken or ways you have contributed to disunity in the body of Christ, decide now to make those relationships right.

If You Are the Offender

Jesus commanded those who have offended others, "If you are offering your gift on the altar, and there you remember that your brother has something against you, leave your gift there in front of the altar. First go and be reconciled with your brother, and then come and offer your gift" (Matt. 5:23-24).

5. REVIEW THE LIST OF RELATIONSHIPS ABOVE. LIST ANY PERSONS OR GROUPS WHOM YOU HAVE OFFENDED BY YOUR SIN AND WHOSE FORGIVENESS AND RECONCILIATION YOU NEED.

Shelly _____   _____
Beth _____   _____

Follow these guidelines to reconcile with those you have offended.

1. Pray and ask God for help in thorough repentance.
2. Go to make things right in obedience to God.
3. Put the most difficult person first on your list.
4. Confess your sin to God and to those directly affected by the sin.
5. Don't apologize. Ask for forgiveness.
6. Go in person (best choice), call by phone (second choice), or write a letter (last resort).
7. Don't reflect negatively on the other person or his actions or attitudes. Deal only with your part of the offense.
8. Make restitution (pay for the offense) when appropriate.
9. Don't expect to receive a positive response every time. Continue to pray for and seek reconciliation with an unforgiving person. Jesus' command is "Be reconciled" (Matt. 5:24).[1]

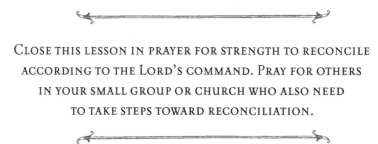

6. WRITE ANY ACTIONS YOU NEED TO TAKE ON "MY PREPARATIONS" LIST ON PAGE 127.

CLOSE THIS LESSON IN PRAYER FOR STRENGTH TO RECONCILE ACCORDING TO THE LORD'S COMMAND. PRAY FOR OTHERS IN YOUR SMALL GROUP OR CHURCH WHO ALSO NEED TO TAKE STEPS TOWARD RECONCILIATION.

---

1. I've been greatly influenced in matters of forgiveness by Life Action Ministries; PO Box 31; Buchanan, MI 49107-0031; www.lifeaction.org.

Tuesday

Day 16 ~ Forgive Those Who Have Offended You

"Whenever you stand praying, if you have anything against anyone, forgive him, so that your Father in heaven will also forgive you your wrongdoing."

Mark 11:25

Going to someone or to a group to ask forgiveness is hard to do. But sometimes the harder work is to forgive those who have offended us. Forgiving someone who has offended us is often very difficult, even for Christians. Nevertheless, God's Word clearly defines our responsibility to forgive those who have hurt us. Notice in Mark 11:25 that we can forgive without even having to go to the person. We can forgive as we "stand praying."

1. LIST BELOW ANY PERSONS OR GROUPS WHOSE SIN HAS OFFENDED YOU. INCLUDE ONLY THOSE WHOM YOU HAVE NOT FORGIVEN OR WITH WHOM THE RELATIONSHIP REMAINS BROKEN. PRAY AND ASK THE LORD TO BRING TO YOUR MIND ANY PERSONS OR GROUPS YOU NEED TO FORGIVE.

⚜ 2. AS YOU READ THE FOLLOWING TRUTHS, DRAW STARS IN THE MARGIN
BESIDE THOSE THAT SEEM PARTICULARLY MEANINGFUL TO YOU.

1. Forgiveness is fully releasing another from the debt of the offense.

2. The person who forgives is the one who has to pay the price of forgiveness, just as Jesus paid the price for you.

3. You are never more like Jesus than when you forgive and show grace and mercy. Being offended provides you with the invitation to reveal Christ to the offender by your forgiveness.

4. Forgiveness does not mean the offense was not wrong.

5. Forgiveness is not permission for the offender to do it again. It does not require you to place yourself in harm's way again.

6. Forgiveness does not mean you will fully forget. However, you choose not to hold the offense against the person any longer.

7. How much do you forgive? Jesus said, "70 times seven" (Matt. 18:22). In other words, forgive an unlimited number of times.

8. Jesus said, "If [your brother] sins against you seven times in a day, and comes back to you seven times, saying, 'I repent,' you must forgive him" (Luke 17:4). In other words, even if the offender really doesn't repent and change his ways, you should still forgive.

9. Even if the person doesn't believe he is wrong, forgive. Jesus set the model for us on the cross when He prayed for those who were killing Him, "Father, forgive them, because they do not know what they are doing" (Luke 23:34).

10. *Forgiveness is releasing the offense into God's hands, knowing He will act in complete justice, mercy, wisdom, etc.*

⚜ 3. REVIEW YOUR LIST ON PAGE 71 OF PERSONS OR GROUPS YOU NEED TO FORGIVE, IF THERE ARE ANY. FOLLOW THESE GUIDELINES TO FORGIVE THOSE WHO HAVE OFFENDED YOU.

1. Forgive the offender. Forgiveness is a command, not an option: "Bear with each other and forgive whatever grievances you may have against one another. Forgive as the Lord forgave you" (Col. 3:13, NIV). "If you don't forgive people, your Father will not forgive your wrongdoing" (Matt. 6:15).

2. You cannot forgive and love in your own strength. The Holy Spirit of Christ in you can enable you to forgive and love. Ask Him to enable you to forgive.

3. Forgiveness is a choice of your will, not the result of a feeling. You must choose to forgive. *– Surrender to God & His wise command.*

4. Begin to pray for God to work in the person's life for his or her good. Continue praying until you can do so with a sincere desire for God to bless the person.

5. Make an investment in the person who wronged you by returning good for evil. Ask God to guide you in this response and in its timing. Ask God what you can do to meet a need or to show love.[1]

CLOSE THIS LESSON BY PRAYING THAT GOD WILL GUIDE YOU
TO FORGIVE AND RECONCILE EVERY BROKEN RELATIONSHIP IN
A WAY THAT WILL BRING HIM GLORY. IF YOU ARE STRUGGLING
WITH FORGIVENESS, CALL A TRUSTED FRIEND AND ASK HIM OR
HER TO PRAY FOR YOU TO BE WILLING AND ABLE TO FORGIVE.
KEEP PRAYING AND FORGIVING UNTIL THE WORK IS DONE.

---

1. Again, I've been greatly influenced in matters of forgiveness by Life Action Ministries; PO Box 31; Buchanan, MI 49107-0031; www.lifeaction.org.

Wensday

Day 17 ~ Restoring Right Relationships

> *"How good and pleasant it is
> when brothers live together in unity!"*
>
> Psalm 133:1, NIV

The lessons for the previous two days may have been some of the most difficult you will ever complete. Reading the lessons and Scriptures is not the end but the beginning. Making relationships right can take time. When I first worked on this message, I was with a church in upstate New York. After the session dealing with broken relationships, a woman came by to speak with me. With tears she said, "I've got so many broken relationships, I can't get them all made right before the Lord's Supper. What should I do?"

We were planning to celebrate the Lord's table the following day. I could tell she had a broken heart over the relationships and a desire to forgive and reconcile. I encouraged her to come because she needed the strength and spiritual nourishment the Lord could give her at His table. Then she would be strong as she began the process of making those relationships right. Fortunately, you have more than one day to work on your relationships!

1. REVIEW DAYS 15 AND 16. PRAY THAT GOD WILL WORK IN YOUR HEART TO ENABLE YOU TO BE RECONCILED AND FORGIVE WHERE NEEDED. OVER THE COMING DAYS, TAKE THE STEPS NECESSARY TO RECONCILE AND FORGIVE. START WITH THE MOST DIFFICULT STEPS OR PERSONS FIRST. START TODAY!

Day 18 ~ Firstborn Among Many Brothers

*"We all, with unveiled faces, are reflecting the glory
of the Lord and are being transformed
into the same image from glory to glory;
this is from the Lord who is the Spirit."*

2 Corinthians 3:18

After the last supper Jesus went to Gethsemane to pray. He was then taken captive, put on trial, crucified the next day, and buried in a borrowed tomb. But on Sunday morning He arose from the grave, the victor over sin and death! Colossians 1:18 describes Jesus as "the beginning, the firstborn from the dead." In Romans 8:29 Paul described Jesus as "the firstborn among many brothers." He is our holy Elder Brother because we have been adopted into God's family as sons and daughters.

1. READ ROMANS 8:28-29 BELOW AND UNDERLINE WHAT GOD PREDESTINED US TO BE.

"We know that all things work together for the good of those who love God: those who are <u>called according to His purpose</u>. For those He foreknew He also <u>predestined to be conformed to the image of His Son</u>, so that He would be the firstborn among many <u>brothers</u>" (Rom. 8:28-29).

God predestined us "to be conformed to the image of his Son" (v. 29). God's determined purpose is that we become like Christ. He uses all of life's experiences—both good and bad—to chip away all the things in us that do not look like Christ so that what remains is like Christ.

Someone once asked a sculptor how he could carve a beautiful angel from a block of marble. He replied, "There is an angel in there. I just chip away everything that is not angel." When you came to faith in Christ, God placed the Holy Spirit of Christ in you. Now He is at work chipping away everything that doesn't look like Christ so that you will be like Him.

2. IN THE FOLLOWING SCRIPTURES UNDERLINE WAYS WE WILL BE LIKE CHRIST. I'VE UNDERLINED THE FIRST ONE FOR YOU.
- "We have the mind of Christ" (1 Cor. 2:16).
- "Just as we have borne the image of the man made of dust, we will also bear the image of the heavenly man" (1 Cor. 15:49).
- "We all, with unveiled faces, are reflecting the glory of the Lord and are being transformed into the same image from glory to glory; this is from the Lord who is the Spirit" (2 Cor. 3:18).
- "[We] have put on the new man, who is being renewed in knowledge according to the image of his Creator" (Col. 3:10).
- "Dear friends, we are God's children now, and what we will be has not yet been revealed. We know that when He appears, we will be like Him, because we will see Him as He is. And everyone who has this hope in Him purifies himself just as He is pure" (1 John 3:2-3).
- "Love is perfected with us so that we may have confidence in the day of judgment; for we are as He is in this world" (1 John 4:17).

3. BASED ON 1 JOHN 3:2-3 ABOVE, BECAUSE WE HAVE THE HOPE OF BEING LIKE CHRIST, WHAT WILL WE DO TO OURSELVES? FILL IN THE BLANKS: "Everyone who has this hope in Him *purifies* himself, just as He is *pure*."

4. BASED ON THESE SCRIPTURES, WHICH OF THE FOLLOWING WILL BE TRUE ABOUT GOD'S CHILDREN? CHECK ONE.
- ❏ a. We will never be like Christ. Our nature is too sinful.
- ☒ b. God is working to make us like Christ. In eternity we will be like Him.

to some degree — all of them ✎

5. GOD IS WORKING TO MAKE YOU LIKE CHRIST. WHAT STILL REMAINS IN YOU THAT MARS (DISTORTS, BLEMISHES, OR HIDES) CHRIST'S IMAGE IN YOU? CHECK ANY THAT APPLY.

❑ Pride/arrogance instead of humility
❑ Disobedience instead of perfect obedience
❑ Love for the world and the things of the world rather than love for God with all your being (heart, soul, mind, and strength)
❑ Lust for influence and power rather than a willingness to be a lowly servant of all
❑ Selfish ambition rather than first seeking His kingdom
❑ Lack of submission to His lordship
❑ Prayerlessness
❑ Lust of the flesh—food, pleasure, sex, etc.
❑ Lust of the eyes
❑ Apathy
❑ Lack of love, compassion
❑ Harshness instead of gentleness
❑ Wanting to rule rather than serve
❑ Selfishness
❑ Unforgiveness
❑ Strife or conflict with others
❑ Lack of submission to Christ, rebellion
❑ Uncontrolled tongue, gossip, slander
❑ Dishonesty/untruthfulness
❑ Lack of mercy
❑ Prejudice
❑ Others: _____

_____

_____

None of us will fully be like Christ this side of heaven. But some Christians have the faulty view that they must continuously live in sin. I've heard Christians say, "I sin every day," as if it were a necessity. The truth is, we can grow in Christlikeness because the Holy Spirit of Christ lives in us to enable our victory over sin.

6. **UNDERLINE WORDS OR PHRASES THAT DESCRIBE OUR NEW RELATIONSHIP TO SIN THAT RESULTED WHEN WE DIED TO OUR OLD SINFUL NATURE AND WERE RAISED TO WALK IN A NEW LIFE IN CHRIST.**

   • "What should we say then? Should we continue in sin in order that grace may multiply? Absolutely not! How can <u>we</u> who <u>died to sin</u> still live in it?" (Rom. 6:1-2).

   • "We know that <u>our old self was crucified with Him</u> in order that <u>sin's dominion over the body may be abolished</u>, so that we may <u>no longer be enslaved to sin</u>, since a person who has died is <u>freed from sin's claims</u>" (Rom. 6:6-7).

   • "<u>Sin will not rule over you</u>, because you are <u>not under law but under grace</u>" (Rom. 6:14).

   • "What then? Should we sin because we are not under law but under grace? Absolutely not! Having been <u>liberated from sin</u>, you became <u>enslaved to righteousness</u>" (Rom. 6:15,18).

   • "Now, since you have been liberated from sin and become enslaved to God, you have your <u>fruit</u>, which results in <u>sanctification</u>—and the end is <u>eternal life</u>!" (Rom. 6:22).

We are dead to sin. Sin is no longer our master; we've been set free from sin. With the power of the indwelling Holy Spirit, we can live as slaves of God and righteousness. Though at times you may fail to live in this victory, it is possible to live increasingly victoriously over sin. Start living up to your birthright!

Throughout our lives <u>God continues His work of molding us into the likeness of His Son. We can cooperate with Him or resist Him</u>. We can cooperate with Him by studying the life of Christ and by allowing the Holy Spirit to conform us to His likeness. We can also cooperate with Him by repenting of sin when He reveals it, returning to the Lord and His ways. Two things can prompt our repentance (turning from sin to God).

7. **UNDERLINE THINGS THAT LEAD TO REPENTANCE.**

   • "Do you despise the riches of His kindness, restraint, and patience, not recognizing that <u>God's kindness</u> is intended to lead you to repentance?" (Rom. 2:4).

   • "<u>Godly grief</u> produces a repentance not to be regretted and leading to salvation, but worldly grief produces death" (2 Cor. 7:10).

One thing that can lead to repentance is <u>godly sorrow</u>—<u>grief over sin that</u> <u>makes you turn from sin to God</u>. Every time you sin, it is as if you drive the nails into Christ's hands, spit on Him, and use the whip on His body. Recognizing this can produce grief and godly sorrow that lead you to repent.

God's kindness can also lead you to repentance. <u>His character of love,</u> <u>mercy, and gentleness can lead you to love and obey Him in response to His</u> <u>undeserved kindness.</u> I pray that this study and the celebration of the Lord's table will increase both your sense of godly sorrow for your sin and your sense of God's unbelievable kindness that He demonstrated at the cross.

8. DO YOU DESIRE TO BE LIKE JESUS? DO YOU YEARN TO LIVE, ACT, AND SPEAK IN A WAY THAT REFLECTS JESUS TO THE WORLD AROUND YOU?   ☒ Yes   ☐ No

9. IF YOU ANSWERED YES, PRAY AND TELL HIM SO.

10. READ THE TEXT OF THE SONG "WHATEVER IT TAKES" ON PAGE 80, UNDERLINING WORDS OR PHRASES THAT DESCRIBE WHAT THE SONG-WRITER IS WILLING TO DO TO DRAW CLOSER AND BE MORE LIKE CHRIST OUR LORD. I'VE UNDERLINED ONE FOR YOU.

11. IN VIEW OF JESUS' DEATH FOR YOU ON THE CROSS, CHECK ITEMS YOU WOULD BE WILLING TO DO TO DRAW CLOSER TO HIM.
☒ He can take (at His request I'll give) the dearest things to me.
☒ I'll accept disappointments, sorrow, and sunless days.
☒ He can have my houses and lands if they are what He wants.
☒ He can change my dreams and my plans.
☒ I'll place my whole life in His hands.
☒ He can call me to go on mission with Him to a faraway land.
☒ I'll trade sunshine for rain.
☒ I'll trade comfort for pain.
☒ I'll do whatever it takes to be more like Him.

We sin because we think the sin will bring about some benefit for us.

Repentance – to turn ① from sin ② to God
Fear of punishment + for negative consequences is a motivation to stop sinning.
But full repentance includes going toward God. seeing His kindness draws us toward Him.

Whatever It Takes

L. W. Wolfe

There's a voice calling me
from an old rugged tree,
And it whispers,
"Draw closer to Me;
Leave this world far behind, there
are new heights to climb,
And a new place in Me
you will find."

For whatever it takes to draw
closer to You, Lord,
That's what I'll be willing to do;
For whatever it takes
to be more like You,
That's what I'll be willing to do.

Take the dearest things to me,
if that's how it must be
To draw me closer to You;

Let the disappointments come,
lonely days without the sun,
If through sorrow more
like You I'll become.

Take my houses and lands, change
my dreams and my plans,
For I'm placing my whole life
in Your hands;
And if You call me today
to a land far away,
Lord, I'll go and Your will obey.

I'll trade sunshine for rain,
comfort for pain,
That's what I'll be willing to do;
For whatever it takes
for my will to break,
That's what I'll be willing to do. [1]

CONCLUDE TODAY'S LESSON IN PRAYER. EXPRESS TO THE LORD
YOUR DESIRE TO BECOME MORE LIKE HIM. GIVE HIM
PERMISSION TO WORK IN YOUR LIFE TO ACCOMPLISH
HIS PERFECT WORK IN YOU. GIVE HIM PERMISSION
TO INCREASE YOUR WILLINGNESS TO SURRENDER
EVERYTHING TO HIS LORDSHIP.

1. "Whatever It Takes," Words and Music by Lanny Wolfe. Copyright © 1975 Lanny Wolfe Music.
All rights controlled by Gaither Copyright Management. Used by permission.

Day 19 ~ Humble Yourself in Servanthood

"'God resists the proud but gives grace
to the humble.' Humble yourselves
therefore under the mighty hand of God,
so that He may exalt you in due time."

1 Peter 5:5-6

On the night of the last supper Jesus gave last-minute lessons and instructions to His disciples. He clearly knew what they would face on the following day. Aware that His remaining days with them would be limited, He prepared to entrust the future of His kingdom to their hands. On that night before the cross, Jesus gave some of His most significant messages to His followers.

On such a somber night and in the presence of the Lord Jesus, an unusual debate arose among the disciples: "A dispute also arose among them about who should be considered the greatest. But He said to them, 'The kings of the Gentiles dominate them, and those who have authority over them are called "Benefactors." But it must not be like that among you. On the contrary, whoever is greatest among you must become like the youngest, and whoever leads, like the one serving. For who is greater, the one at the table or the one serving? Isn't it the one at the table? But I am among you as the One who serves'" (Luke 22:24-27).

1. WHAT WERE THE DISCIPLES ARGUING ABOUT? Which of them would be the *greatest*

2. HOW DO THE KINGS OF THE GENTILES RELATE TO THEIR SUBJECTS?

dominate them

3. HOW DO THOSE WHO CALL THEMSELVES BENEFACTORS RELATE?

forced authority

4. WHAT SHOULD THE GREATEST AMONG CHRIST'S DISCIPLES BE LIKE?

to serve – meeting needs

5. HOW SHOULD A DISCIPLE LEAD? *by serving, meeting needs*

Jesus the Savior, the King of kings, the Creator of the heavens and earth, the Ruler of the universe, was in the room with them, and the disciples were arguing about who would be the greatest. How disoriented they were to Christ and His kingdom work. How arrogant they were to argue about their own greatness in the presence of the King. And this was not the first time Jesus had had to correct them. The disciples had had this argument at least once before (see Matt. 20:20-28), but they still didn't understand.

Earthly human rulers demand that people submit to their position or authority. They use their power, position, or influence to exercise authority and pressure others to follow. Often they act in a demanding or dictatorial manner. They arrogantly look down on the ones they rule as ignorant and inferior. Jesus made it clear that this was not the way to be great in His kingdom. Greatness would come through humility and servanthood.

Jesus offered Himself as their model: "I am among you as the One who serves" (v. 27). On this very night after the meal, Jesus took a towel and basin of water and washed the disciples' dirty feet (see John 13:2-17). He said to them, "You call Me Teacher and Lord. This is well said, for I am. So if I, your Lord and Teacher, have washed your feet, you also ought to wash one another's feet. For I have given you an example that you also should do just as I have done for you" (John 13:13-15).

6. WHEN YOU ARE IN A PLACE OF LEADERSHIP AROUND GOD'S
   PEOPLE—AT CHURCH, ON A COMMITTEE OR BOARD, IN A CLASS,
   OR EVEN AT HOME—WHICH STYLE OF LEADERSHIP DO YOU TEND
   TO USE? HONESTLY CHECK ONE. IF YOU PREFER, WRITE A LIST
   OF YOUR OWN WORDS TO DESCRIBE YOUR LEADERSHIP.

   ❑ a. Proud, arrogant, forceful, throw my weight around, manipula-
   tive, argumentative, claim my rights, exercise authority, demanding, impatient, unyielding, uncompromising, condescending,
   critical

   ❑ b. Humble, gentle, understanding, patient, cooperative, a listener,
   teachable, correctable, willing to lay down my rights or opinion for the sake of the body of Christ, point others to Christ's
   leadership, prayerful, a servant of the body

   ❑ c. My own list: _____

   _____

I am grieved and distressed by the conflict in many churches today. Division
abounds. Pastors, staff, committees, boards, elders, deacons, and sometimes
the entire congregation are in turmoil. Groups are polarized. Pastors and
staff are fired. Angry members leave the church, sometimes in a large church
split. Members have very little love for one another—a love that seeks the
best for the others. Often the issue is the same one the disciples were arguing
about at the last supper (see Luke 22:24-27). God's people are fighting over
who will be the greatest, who will be in control, who will get to have their
way, who will win. When the church of the living Christ acts this way, we
disgrace the name of Christ and bring reproach on His kingdom.

Pride is a root sin. When it is strong in your life, it can lead to or encourage other sins, like being argumentative, boastfulness, complaining, having
a critical spirit, being demanding, disobedience, exalting self, faultfinding,
gossiping, haughtiness, impatience, independence, ingratitude, pleasing
people instead of God, prejudice, rudeness, stubbornness, being unforgiving, prayerlessness, self-righteousness, self-sufficiency, having selfish
ambition, self-promotion, having a judgmental spirit, sexual immorality,
taking license to sin, rebellion toward authority, desiring or demanding
control, following your own evil desires, thinking more highly of self, or
being unrepentant and holding on to sin.

❧ 7. READ THE PREVIOUS PARAGRAPH AGAIN AND CIRCLE ANY SINS THAT MAY INDICATE THE PRESENCE OF PRIDE IN YOUR LIFE.

❧ 8. WOULD YOU HAVE TO CONFESS THAT YOU HAVE TOO MUCH PRIDE IN YOUR LIFE? ☒ Yes ☐ No

❧ 9. READ WHAT GOD SAYS ABOUT PRIDE. CIRCLE THE WORD *pride* OR *proud* EACH TIME IT OCCURS.

- "The LORD preserves the faithful,
  but the proud he pays back in full" (Ps. 31:23, NIV).
- "Though the LORD is on high, he looks upon the lowly,
  the proud he knows from afar" (Ps. 138:6, NIV).
- "I hate arrogant pride, evil conduct,
  and perverse speech" (Prov. 8:13).
- "Everyone with a proud heart is detestable to the LORD;
  be assured, he will not go unpunished" (Prov. 16:5).
- "Pride comes before destruction,
  and an arrogant spirit before a fall" (Prov. 16:18).
- "I will put an end to the pride of the arrogant
  and humiliate the insolence of tyrants" (Isa. 13:11).
- "God resists the proud, but gives grace to the humble.
  Humble yourselves therefore under the mighty hand of God,
  so that He may exalt you in due time" (1 Pet. 5:5-6).

Have you ever stopped to think that opposition, resistance, humiliation, and punishment can be God's doing and not just spiritual warfare? Many Christians blame the Devil for these things when they can be God's work because of pride in His children.

❧ 10. IN THE LAST SCRIPTURE ABOVE, PETER GIVES YOU A WAY TO COMBAT PRIDE IN YOUR LIFE. WHAT ARE YOU TO DO TO YOURSELF?

humble myself

When you humble yourself before God, He can gain glory for Himself through your life. He Himself will lift you up in due time. God tells us another value to being humble, lowly, and contrite: "This is what the high and lofty One says—he who lives forever, whose name is holy: 'I live in a high and holy place, but also with him who is contrite and lowly in spirit, to revive the spirit of the lowly and to revive the heart of the contrite'" (Isa. 57:15, NIV). God chooses to live with those who are contrite and lowly in spirit. Those are the ones He chooses to revive. Let's humble ourselves individually and ← as churches corporately so that we can experience revival.

The big question becomes, How do I humble myself? The sin of pride normally cannot be dealt with privately because its very nature encourages you to keep quiet about it. Refusing to confess the sin of pride to God and others may strengthen the pride in you rather than ruthlessly deal with it. Watch for or even seek opportunities to acknowledge your pride to a brother or sister in Christ and ask him or her to pray for you. Such a confession might even be appropriate in a group setting. Humility was a distinguishing mark of Jesus Christ: He "made himself nothing, taking the very nature of a servant" and "humbled himself and became obedient to death—even death on a cross!" (Phil. 2:7-8, NIV). When Christ's humility begins to pervade your life, you will bring Him glory and honor.

When you humble yourself, God develops a spirit of humility in your character. The alternative is to let the Lord humiliate you. Let me suggest some actions that can be humbling.

11. CHECK ACTIONS THAT WOULD HELP YOU DEVELOP HUMILITY.
- ☒ Acknowledge God's greatness and sovereignty.
- ☒ Give all credit and glory to Christ.
- ☒ Agree with God about your sin; repent of sin.
- ☒ Give up or yield your rights.
- ☒ Lead from a position of loving service to those you lead.
- ☒ Lay down your plans, dreams, opinions, and preferences for those of others.
- ☒ Yield a position of authority to another, if God so directs.
- ☒ Assume a subordinate role.
- ☒ Serve others.
- ☒ Accept lowly tasks without complaint.
- ☒ Perform lowly tasks well.
- ☒ Publicly confess sin when appropriate.
- ☒ Confess your weaknesses or needs and accept help.
- ☒ Submit to those in authority over you without complaint.

☒ Secretly fast in brokenness.
☒ Obey God even when it doesn't make sense or is costly.
☒ Yield to the desires or wishes of subordinates.
☒ Lift up others above yourself.
☒ Accept humiliating circumstances as valuable lessons.
☒ Confess dependence on God and interdependence on others.
☒ Honor others above yourself.
☒ Do the things pride tells you not to do. ←
☒ Ask critics and contenders to pray for you.
☒ Deny your selfish desires.
☒ Give away or dispose of things that cause you to feel proud.
☒ Ask for help. Receive help from others when you need help.
☒ Express your needs.
☒ Allow others to "wash your feet."
☒ Ask others to pray for you.
☒ Place yourself before God as utterly helpless.
☒ Agree with Christ that apart from Him you can do nothing.
☒ Accept invitations to take a lowly place.
☒ Yield control to others. *appropriately*.
☒ Give to the needy.
☒ Be willing to associate with people of low degree.
☒ Submit to one another in reverence for Christ.
☒ Look out for the needs of others rather than your own.
☒ Surrender to God's will.
☒ Look up at the infinite God and see how small you are.
☒ Anonymously do things for others.
☒ Accept and perform menial tasks without complaint.

PRAY, RUTHLESSLY DEALING WITH ANY EVIDENCE OF PRIDE IN
YOUR LIFE. THEN REVIEW THE PREVIOUS LIST OF ACTIONS AND
ASK THE LORD TO GUIDE YOU INTO SPECIFIC WAYS TO HUMBLE
YOURSELF. CIRCLE THE ACTIONS HE HIGHLIGHTS FOR YOU.

12. TURN TO "MY PREPARATIONS" LIST ON PAGE 127 AND LIST ANY
ACTIONS YOU NEED TO TAKE IN PREPARATION FOR THE LORD'S TABLE.

Saturday

Day 20 ~ Love One Another

"This is how we have come to know love:
He laid down His life for us. We should
also lay down our lives for our brothers."

1 John 3:16

God loved you and me so much that He gave His only Son to pay the necessary death penalty for our sin. He loved us and met our need for a Savior. At the last supper with His disciples, Jesus gave us a new commandment: "I give you a new commandment: love one another. Just as I have loved you, you must also love one another. By this all people will know that you are My disciples, if you have love for one another" (John 13:34-35). Jesus gave us the example of love. As we reflect that same love to our fellow Christians, the world will recognize that we are disciples (followers) of Jesus Christ. Love is a choice you make to seek the best for another person. How do you show love to one another? The Apostle John gives us some answers.

1. READ THE FOLLOWING TWO SCRIPTURES AND UNDERLINE WAYS WE CAN SHOW LOVE TO OUR BROTHERS AND SISTERS IN CHRIST.
   + "This is how we have come to know love: He laid down His life for us. We should also <u>lay down our lives for our brothers</u>" (1 John 3:16).
   + "If anyone has this world's goods and <u>sees</u> his brother in need but shuts off his compassion from him—how can God's love

reside in him? Little children, we must not love in word or speech, but in deed and truth" (1 John 3:17-18).

We show love by meeting needs. Love is not a feeling or words; it is an action that meets a need. We can also show love by laying down our lives for our brothers. Most of us will read that verse and assume it doesn't apply to us because we will not likely be asked to lay down our physical lives. Don't pass over it too quickly.

I was leading revival services in a church that was deeply divided over a number of issues. One issue was the style of worship music used in the Sunday services. Some wanted to return to the traditional use of a hymnal led by a music leader. Others enjoyed the use of praise choruses displayed by an overhead projector and led by a praise team. I spoke on loving one another enough to lay down yourself in love for your brothers and sisters in Christ. I didn't suggest any specifics, but I said we can lay down our personal opinions, preferences, desires, plans, dreams, and things from love for others.

The next night the leader of the praise team came to me. She said God had convicted her in the service the night before that the praise team needed to lay down their music leadership from love for the rest of the body. When she called the other team members, God had said the same thing to them as well. That night they all came at the invitation time, publicly resigned, and asked forgiveness for causing division in the body. They said, "We love you too much to continue being a source of division. We are laying down the praise team because we love you." That is love in action, not just in words.

Divisions in a church over worship style indicate that worship is tending toward ritual rather than a genuine encounter with the living God. In this case the issue was not whether one style of music leadership was better than the other. As far as the Lord is concerned, either would be acceptable if the hearts are right. The issue was that people were holding on to their own personal preferences and dividing the body of Christ rather than showing love. Either side could have laid down its preferences from love for the body, and God would have been pleased. Unity and love are important to God.

Ask God to reveal anything He wants you to lay down from love for your brothers and sisters in Christ. If an area of division exists between you and other believers, ask the Lord how you can show your love in actions rather than just in words. If you know a believer who has a need, ask God what, if anything, He wants you to lay down to meet that need.

2. Does God want you to lay down or give away any of the following? Check any that He speaks to you about or write your own.

- ❑ A material possession
- ❑ Your preferences
- ❑ Your dream or goal
- ❑ An attitude
- ❑ A schedule
- ❑ A position of leadership
- ❑ Resistance to change
- ❑ Opposition to a project
- ❑ Withholding of support
- ❑ Your reputation

- ❑ Money
- ❑ Your opinion
- ❑ Your desires
- ❑ A behavior
- ❑ An activity
- ❑ Time to serve others
- ❑ Your comfort or security
- ☒ Your expectations
- ❑ Your rights
- ❑ Your life, if God asks for it

☒ *Consistent kindness* _____

❑ _____

❑ _____

Pray that God will help your church members truly love one another.

Day 21 ~ Group Session 3

OPEN WITH PRAYER

Invite volunteers to pray sentence prayers of confession, praise, thanksgiving, or petition in response to what God has done in their lives this week.

REVIEW DAYS 15–20

1. What Scripture, statement, idea, testimony, or illustration that you read this week was most significant or meaningful to you and why?
2. How is your fellowship with God affected when you fail to reconcile or forgive?
3. How should a person respond if he realizes he has offended someone else? What steps could he take?
4. How should a person respond if she realizes she has been offended by someone else? What steps could she take?
5. What does the Bible say about God's intention for us to become like Jesus?
6. What are some characteristics of Jesus that God wants to be true of you?
7. What are two things that lead us to repentance? (See day 18, activity 7, p. 78.) Give an example of each.
8. What is evidence of pride in a person's life? What is evidence of humility in a person's life?

SING/LISTEN

Select a song or hymn that focuses your attention on Christ and His sacrifice on the cross. Sing it together, read the lyrics, or listen to someone sing it live or from a recording. If you have a recording of "Whatever It Takes" (see p. 80), you may want to play or sing along with it to reinforce your surrender to become more like Jesus.

RESPOND TO LEARNING ACTIVITIES

1. Day 16, activity 2 (p. 72). Which truth about forgiveness was most meaningful or helpful to you and why?
2. Day 18, activity 6 (p. 78). According to Romans 6, how is a Christian related to sin?
3. Day 19, activity 11 (p. 85). What are you willing to do to become more like Jesus? Which of those things will be the most difficult?
4. Day 19, activity 11 (p. 85). What actions will help you develop greater humility and why?
5. Day 20, activity 2 (p. 89). What, if anything, do you sense God wants you to lay down or give away because of your love for others?

PRAY TOGETHER

1. Divide into small groups (three to five) of the same gender. Ask each person, In which area do you need the greatest help in preparing for the Lord's table (or in which area are you having the greatest difficulty)? Share specific prayer requests for that area of need or difficulty and pray for one another. Possible areas:
   - Reconciling relationships
   - Forgiving others
   - Becoming like Jesus
   - Developing humility
   - Loving others
2. In a large group invite volunteers to pray for your church in relationship to the topics you have examined this week.

PREPARE FOR THE LORD'S TABLE

1. Discuss your church's plans for observing the Lord's table. If you have plans for a pre-Communion service or a love feast, review the plans, dates, and any preparation required.
2. If your church plans to receive a special love offering, share information about how the offering will be used and pray that the Lord will be pleased and honored by the loving responses of His people.

PREVIEW THE COMING WEEK

Day 22 ~ A Love Relationship with the Father

> *"Jesus answered, 'If anyone loves Me, he will keep My word. My Father will love him, and We will come to him and make Our home with him.'"*
>
> John 14:23

When Jesus died, He paid the penalty for our sin and made forgiveness available to us. We all need that forgiveness. Some need to know His healing touch as well. In today's lesson I want to address spiritual healing that you may need.

Some Christians do not experience the full dimensions of a love relationship with God. They want to love God and be loved by Him, but they consciously or subconsciously keep Him at a distance. They never seem to experience a closeness to God as their Heavenly Father. Sometimes they get very involved in church activities seeking an experience of God's love that seems elusive.

1. HOW WOULD YOU DESCRIBE YOUR EXPERIENCE OF AN INTIMATE LOVE RELATIONSHIP WITH YOUR HEAVENLY FATHER? CHECK ONE OR WRITE YOUR OWN.
   - ☒ a. I've experienced a close, personal, loving relationship with Him.
   - ❏ b. I've felt a longing for that love and closeness, but I can't ever seem to experience that relationship with Him.

❑ c. For some reason I fear God and will not allow Him to get close to me. It's as if I say, "God, I want You to love me, but don't come too close."

❑ d. My knowledge of God's love has been almost exclusively a head knowledge. I've never sought a personal relationship.

❑ e. Other: _____

_____

If you checked a, you may want to skip to day 23. If you have not experienced a closeness to your Heavenly Father, the problem could be sin in your life. If that is the case, you need to repent and return to Him. The lessons the past two weeks were designed to help you do that. I've encountered a variety of other reasons for this sense of distance from God:

- One or both parents were verbally, physically, or sexually abusive.
- A parent (especially a father) was not present to show love because of death, abandonment, divorce, or physical disability.
- One or both parents neglected a child because of work commitments, drug or alcohol abuse, or emotional problems.
- A spiritual leader or a significant other person was emotionally, physically, or sexually abusive.

In these cases your problem may stem from others' sin, not your own. Or it may not be anyone's sin but unfortunate circumstances. If you respond to these circumstances by sinning, you need to confront your sin. We dealt with that subject in days 15 and 16, which addressed reconciling and forgiving. But you may also have a wounded spirit that needs to be healed. You need to experience not only Jesus' forgiveness but also His healing touch. Perhaps you are spiritually needy, just as the woman in the following Scripture was physically needy: "Just then, a woman who had suffered from bleeding for 12 years approached from behind and touched the tassel on His robe, for she said to herself, 'If I can just touch His robe, I'll be made well!' But Jesus turned and saw her. 'Have courage, daughter,' He said. 'Your faith has made you well.' And the woman was made well from that moment" (Matt. 9:20-22).

2. Do you sense a need for spiritual healing that you know only Jesus can give? ❏ Yes ❏ No

> If so, even if you cannot explain or identify the reason for your need, ask the Lord to act as your Great Physician and do the healing work He knows you need. Check here if you prayed and asked for His healing touch: ❏

I spoke to a woman who had been abused as a child and kept God at a distance because of her fears. She needed to know God's safe, pure, gentle, trustworthy love. She knew about His love in her head, but she needed to experience His love so that she would know it in her heart. God had permitted her to be overwhelmed with problems. This was an ideal time for her to experience His love.

We prayed, and I recommended that she go alone to her Heavenly Father, drop her guard, and allow Him to love her. I didn't know how He might do that, but I knew He was the only One who could reveal His love in the way she needed it. I couldn't explain His love more completely than she already knew intellectually.

She came back the next day to tell me her story. She spent the afternoon in a garden alone with her Heavenly Father. He revealed His love to her in such a way that she was overwhelmed by peace and comfort. Months later she told me that she felt as if God had given her a heart transplant.

On another occasion I spoke with a woman whose father had been a workaholic and had never had time for her. She was having difficulty feeling close to her Heavenly Father while worshiping. As we talked, she described her regular desire to pray. When I prayed with her, I asked the Lord something I had never prayed before. I said, "Lord, Your Word says that because of sin, no one seeks You. Because my sister is sensing a desire to pray, that must be Your invitation for her to spend time with You. Would You help her interpret her every desire to pray as Your invitation for a Father-daughter date?"

After the prayer I explained that her Heavenly Father dearly loved her, wanted to spend time with His daughter, and wanted to reveal His love to her. Months later I received a letter from her that said, "I've had many Father-daughter dates since we talked. It's been wonderful! And now when I worship, I feel a deep love for God because I have experienced His love for me."

If you have difficulty experiencing a closeness to your Heavenly Father, understand that He wants to reveal His love to you more than you want to experience it. You need to let Him.

3. PLAN A FATHER-DAUGHTER DATE (FOR GIRLS/WOMEN) OR A FATHER-SON OUTING (FOR BOYS/MEN). SPEND THIS TIME WITH YOUR HEAVENLY FATHER AS SOON AS YOU CAN SET ASIDE THE TIME. TRY TO SCHEDULE IT IN THE NEXT WEEK OR TWO WHILE THE EXPERIENCE OF THE LORD'S TABLE IS FRESH ON YOUR MIND.

- Go to a favorite spot or a quiet place where you can be alone with your Father (perhaps an outdoor place). Allow for an extended period of time—an hour or maybe several hours.
- Don't worry about what to say. God's love is unconditional. Your experience of His love does not depend on your praying the right prayer, claiming the right promise, or quoting the right Scripture. Just get alone with Him and let Him love you.
- If you've been wounded in the past, tell your Father about the pain. Let Him lance the wound in your spirit and drain the corruption that has collected there. Ask Him to heal the wound and take away the pain. Remember:

> *There is a balm in Gilead to make the wounded whole;*
> *There is a balm in Gilead to heal the sin-sick soul.* [1]

- Ask Him to forgive you and cleanse you of any bitterness, unforgiveness, or sin on your own part. Ask Him for help to forgive anyone who has offended you. Jesus can help you do this.
- Give Him permission to reveal His love to you in any way He chooses. Become like a child again. Allow your Heavenly Father to wrap His loving arms around you and hold you close. Receive His love.
- Every time you feel a desire to pray or a desire to spend time with Him, interpret that as His invitation for time with you, His child. Give Him all the time He wants. He will fill the emptiness or void in your life. His love is sufficient.
- Understand that experiencing God's love may involve a process over a period of time and not just an event when God breaks

through. Let God do the work on His timetable. He loves you; He will not leave you like an orphan. Give Him time to do His work.

4. WRITE A BRIEF ACCOUNT OF YOUR TIME ALONE WITH YOUR HEAVENLY FATHER. RECORD WAYS HE REVEALS HIS LOVE TO YOU, THINGS YOU HAVE TALKED (PRAYED) ABOUT, FEELINGS OF COMFORT AND HEALING, AND SO FORTH. USE EXTRA PAPER IF NEEDED.

_____

_____

_____

_____

_____

_____

_____

_____

_____

_____

PRAY ABOUT YOUR UPCOMING TIME WITH YOUR HEAVENLY FATHER OR THANK HIM FOR WHAT YOU HAVE ALREADY EXPERIENCED OF HIS LOVE IN TIMES ALONE WITH HIM.

1. "There Is a Balm in Gilead," *The Baptist Hymnal* (Nashville: Convention Press, 1991), 269.

Tuesday

Day 23 ~ A Walk to Emmaus

"Weren't our hearts ablaze within us while He was talking with us on the road and explaining the Scriptures to us?"

Luke 24:32

Following His resurrection, Jesus took a walk with two persons who had been in Jerusalem during the crucifixion. On the road their hearts burned!

1. Read their story in Luke 24:13-35 and think what it must have been like to have their hearts "ablaze" as Jesus talked with them and explained the Scriptures.

2. Take a walk and have a talk with your Lord (or find a quiet place to sit and talk with Him). Too often our prayer times are hurried or filled with requests. Try to get away from your busy world and spend half an hour or more with Jesus with no set agenda. Just spend time talking with Him as a friend who has given His life for you. <u>Enjoy His presence</u>. Before you go, read or sing "In the Garden" on page 98 and then go with Him to your special place.

In the Garden

C. Austin Miles

I come to the garden alone,
While the dew is still on the roses;
And the voice I hear,
falling on my ear,
The Son of God discloses.

He speaks, and the sound
of His voice
Is so sweet the birds
hush their singing;
And the melody
that He gave to me
Within my heart is ringing.

Refrain
And He walks with me,
and He talks with me,
And He tells me I am His own,
And the joy we share
as we tarry there,
None other has ever known.

3. AFTER YOUR TIME ALONE WITH JESUS, REFLECT ON YOUR EXPERI-
ENCE. SUMMARIZE YOUR THOUGHTS OR FEELINGS BELOW.

He - God Himself! - loves - me

He is meek and lowly in heart!

Day 24 ~ Forgiveness and Love

> *"Her many sins have been forgiven;*
> *that's why she loved much.*
> *But the one who is forgiven little, loves little."*
>
> Luke 7:47

Jesus went to a Pharisee's house for a meal. While they were eating, "a woman in the town who was a sinner" (Luke 7:37) anointed Jesus' feet with perfume and wiped them with her hair. Simon the Pharisee thought Jesus should have rejected her because of her sinful past. Jesus told him this parable:

> "A creditor had two debtors. One owed 500 denarii, and the other 50. Since they could not pay it back, he graciously forgave them both. So, which of them will love him more?"
>
> Simon answered, "I suppose the one he forgave more."
>
> "You have judged correctly," He told him. Turning to the woman, He said to Simon, "Do you see this woman? I entered your house; you gave Me no water for My feet, but she, with her tears, has washed My feet and wiped them with her hair. You gave Me no kiss, but she hasn't stopped kissing My feet since I came in. You didn't anoint My head with oil, but she has anointed My feet with fragrant oil. Therefore I tell you, her many sins have been forgiven; that's why she loved much. But the one who is forgiven little, loves little" (Luke 7:41-47).

COME TO THE LORD'S TABLE

1. THINK ABOUT YOUR LIFE OF SIN, YOUR REBELLION AGAINST GOD, YOUR NEGLECT OF HIM, OR YOUR REPEATED OFFENSES THAT HE HAS FORGIVEN. WHICH OF THE FOLLOWING CHOICES BEST DESCRIBES YOUR LOVE FOR GOD? CHECK ONE OR WRITE YOUR OWN.

☒ a. I've been forgiven so much that I can't help but love Him deeply.

❑ b. I don't think He's had to forgive me very much, and my love for Him is shallow.

☒ c. Just knowing He gave His life for me causes me to love Him greatly.

❑ d. For some reason I do not feel much love toward Christ.

❑ e. Other: _____

We are the recipients of God's love, which He demonstrated to us through Christ and His death on the cross. What a great love! We've been forgiven. Our sin debt has been paid. If your love for Him is small, I pray that God will open your eyes to see the greatness of the love He has lavished on you and that He will enable you to know His love by experience. If you love Him much, you will want to express that love. But Jesus is in heaven. How can you express your love for Him? Jesus described judgment day, when the King will commend His "sheep":

> The King will say to those on His right, "Come, you who are blessed by My Father, inherit the kingdom prepared for you from the foundation of the world.
>> *For I was hungry*
>> *and you gave Me something to eat;*
>> *I was thirsty*
>> *and you gave Me something to drink;*
>> *I was a stranger and you took Me in;*
>> *I was naked and you clothed Me;*
>> *I was sick and you took care of Me;*
>> *I was in prison and you visited Me."*
>
> Then the righteous will answer Him, "Lord, when did we see You hungry and feed You, or thirsty and give You something to drink? When did we see You a stranger and take You in, or without clothes and clothe You? When did we see You sick, or in prison, and visit You?"

And the King will answer them, "I assure you: Whatever you did for one of the least of these brothers of Mine, you did for Me" (Matt. 25:34-40).

One way you can express your love for Jesus is by loving others. <u>Watch for ways you can show love for others by meeting their needs</u>.

2. READ THE FOLLOWING LIST OF NEEDS. IF A PERSON OR GROUP WITH SUCH A NEED COMES TO MIND, CHECK THE BOX AND WRITE THE PERSON'S OR GROUP'S NAME OR INITIALS BESIDE THE BOX.

❑ Assistance in working through governmental red tape
❑ Basic human needs like food, water, clothes, or shelter
☒ Basic skills training such as reading, math, verbal, parenting, computer, or other job skills
☒ Break from overwhelming child-care pressures
❑ Car repair
☒ Comfort in a time of grief
❑ Defense against oppression
☒ Encouragement to break free from a destructive habit
❑ Financial counseling or money-management skills
❑ Financial resources to provide for basic family needs
☒ Friendship, companionship, attention
❑ Health or dental care
☒ Help in reconciling a broken relationship with someone
☒ Help with child care
❑ Help with house or lawn work due to physical limitations
❑ Job or employment opportunity
❑ Justice
❑ Learning English as a second language
❑ Manual help to do a job the person cannot do alone
❑ Marriage counseling or enrichment
☒ Material things the person needs but can't afford
❑ Opportunity to experience success or personal fulfillment
☒ Prayer for a felt need
☒ Protection and security from an unsafe environment
☒ Someone to talk to, confide in, or seek counsel from
☒ Time for husband and wife to get away from the children

☒ Transportation
❏ Tutoring for GED
☒ Visit when they are in the hospital, nursing home, or prison
☒ Wise counsel for critical decision making

Review the items you checked. Pray and ask the Lord to reveal times and ways you can demonstrate your love for Him by loving others. Write any actions He guides you to take on "My Preparations" list on page 127.

In day 20 you examined Jesus' command to love one another. Is your church planning a love feast at the conclusion of this study? If so, you may have been asked to consider giving a special thank or love offering. This will be an opportunity for you to give an extra special offering to say, "Thank You, Jesus, for giving Your life for me!" We can never repay Him, but we can express our love by loving those for whom He died. This offering should be freely given or not at all. It should be in addition to your regular tithe and other gifts to God's work. If God identified a heart idol you need to give away (see day 12), you may want to give it or sell it and give the proceeds as a part of your love offering.

3. If your church plans to receive a love offering, prayerfully think about what you would like to give. If your church is not receiving an offering, think of another way to express your love to Christ and others through a special gift. What, if anything, have you decided to give?

_____

Close today's lesson with a prayer of thanksgiving. Express to Jesus your love for Him because of the forgiveness He has given you.

Day 25 ~ Love and Obedience

"If you love Me, you will keep My commandments."

John 14:15

We're drawing near to the time for the Lord's table. I pray that God has rekindled in you a first love for Christ. He longs to draw you closer.

1. IF YOU STILL FIND THAT YOUR LOVE FOR THE LORD IS NOT WHAT IT SHOULD BE, CONTINUE TO SEEK HIM THROUGH THE FOLLOWING ACTIONS. WRITE SPECIFIC ACTIONS ON PAGE 127.
   + Spend time with your Lord. Take some more walks with Him.
   + Ask Him to reveal His love to you in such a way that you will know His love by experience.
   + Spend time reviewing days 2–8 to know Jesus' sacrificial love for you on the cross.
   + Review days 9–20 and seek to get right in your relationships with the Lord and others.
   + Begin to obey Him.

The final suggestion in this list, obedience, is directly connected to your love for the Lord.

2. READ THE FOLLOWING SCRIPTURES AND CIRCLE THE WORDS *love, loves, loved, obey,* AND *obeys* EACH TIME THEY OCCUR.
   - "If you love me, you will obey what I command" (John 14:15, NIV).
   - "Whoever has my commands and obeys them, he is the one who loves me. He who loves me will be loved by my Father, and I too will love him and show myself to him" (John 14:21, NIV).
   - "If anyone loves me, he will obey my teaching. My Father will love him, and we will come to him and make our home with him. He who does not love me will not obey my teaching" (John 14:23-24, NIV).

3. WHAT WILL THE ONE WHO LOVES JESUS DO WITH HIS COMMANDS (SEE V. 21)? *obeys*

4. IF YOU LOVE AND OBEY JESUS, HOW WILL HE AND THE FATHER RESPOND TO YOU (SEE VV. 23-24)?

He will love him, come to him, "make our home w/ him."

When you love Jesus, you obey what He commands. When you love and obey Him, Jesus reveals Himself to you, and He and the Father take up residence in your life in a new way. Obedience is a characteristic of Jesus Himself. He said, "My food is to do the will of Him who sent Me and to finish His work" (John 4:34). Paul said about Jesus,

> He humbled Himself by becoming obedient
> to the point of death—even to death on a cross (Phil. 2:8).

When you love Jesus and seek to live like Him, you obey Him.

The Final Command

After Jesus' resurrection He spent 40 days instructing His disciples. On several occasions He commanded them to carry the good news of salvation to all peoples of the earth. He wanted to make sure His disciples did not miss His final command, because all His ministry and sacrifice would be wasted if they failed to obey Him.

✥ 5. READ AND UNDERLINE JESUS' FINAL COMMAND BELOW.
"<u>Go, therefore, and make disciples of all nations, baptizing them in the</u> <u>name of the Father and of the Son and of the Holy Spirit, teaching</u> <u>them to observe everything I have commanded you</u>" (Matt. 28:19-20).

Just before Jesus ascended into heaven, He reminded His disciples one more time: "You will receive power when the Holy Spirit has come upon you, and you will be My witnesses in Jerusalem, in all Judea and Samaria, and to the ends of the earth" (Acts 1:8). Why should we, as His present-day disciples, obey this final command? Paul wrote to the Corinthian church about the ministry God has assigned to us to reconcile people to God.

✥ 6. IN 2 CORINTHIANS 5:14-15 UNDERLINE THE REASON WE SHOULD
GIVE OURSELVES TO THE TASK OF HELPING OTHERS KNOW CHRIST.
"Christ's love <u>compels</u> us, since we have reached this conclusion:
if One died for all, then all died. And He died for all so that those
who live should no longer live for themselves, but for the One who
died for them and was raised" (2 Cor. 5:14-15).

Christ's love for us compels us to love Him and to carry His message of reconciliation to others.

✥ 7. FROM YOUR LOVE FOR YOUR LORD, WILL YOU PRAY AND SURRENDER
YOURSELF TO OBEY THE FINAL COMMAND? ☒ Yes ☐ No

If you will, <u>God will help you know what your part is</u>. Work together with your church to reap the harvest Christ says is already ripe (see Luke 10:2). From our love for Christ let's adopt the battle cry of Moravian missions: "To win for the Lamb that was slain, the reward of His sufferings."[1]

PRAY ABOUT THE LORD'S FINAL COMMAND AND ASK HOW YOU
ARE TO BE INVOLVED. PLEDGE YOUR LOVE AND OBEDIENCE.

---

1. Andrew Murray, *The Key to the Missionary Problem* (New York: The American Tract Society, 1901), 37.

Day 26 ~ Pre-Communion Meditations

*"[Jesus] said to them, 'I have fervently desired
to eat this Passover with you before I suffer.
For I tell you, I will not eat it again
until it is fulfilled in the kingdom of God.'"*

Luke 22:15

As the time for the Lord's table draws near, let's focus our attention on the Lord and the supper.

1. WHICH OF THE FOLLOWING STATEMENTS BEST DESCRIBES YOUR THOUGHTS AND EMOTIONS AS YOU APPROACH THE LORD'S TABLE? CHECK ONE OR WRITE YOUR OWN.
   ❑ a. I have never taken the Lord's table so seriously. Now that I am prepared, I am eager to meet my Lord at His table.
   ❑ b. God has revealed so much that has been hidden in my heart or that I've tolerated in my life, I tremble at the thought of meeting Him at His table.
   ❑ c. God has revealed so many broken relationships in my life that I know I can't get everything reconciled before the supper. I question whether I should come to the table.
   ❑ d. You've blown this emphasis way out of proportion. Don't expect me to get too serious about the Lord's table.
   ❑ e. Other: _____

I pray that our study together has helped you better prepare to partake of the Lord's table in a worthy manner. Perhaps you feel overwhelmed by the task of getting your relationships right with God and with others. You may even have thoughts of not attending the service because of the ways the Holy Spirit has convicted you this week. If you are that serious about getting your life right with the Lord, then the Lord's table is probably just the place for you.

Jesus knows your weakness, your need, and your heart. Do you remember what He said to the woman caught in adultery? "'Neither do I condemn you,' Jesus declared. 'Go, and from now on do not sin anymore'" (John 8:11). He doesn't invite you to the table to condemn you. He is always ready to welcome a repentant sinner. If you have put on Christ in salvation, He becomes your wedding garment. You are welcome at His table. Remember that Jesus said, "I have fervently desired to eat this Passover with you" (Luke 22:15). He is looking forward to your presence at the table. Jesus invites you to come.

Do you need a fresh cleansing from sin and unrighteousness? Come! Are you weary and burdened? Come! Do you want to follow Christ so that you will experience the abundant life He came to give? Come! Do you hunger and thirst for more in your life and in your experience of God? Come! The Lord has spiritual food and drink waiting at His table. The needy are welcome there. Come to the Lord's table! He will satisfy your soul.

The following are two meditations from Andrew Murray's The Lord's Table. I pray that these thoughts will bless you as you prepare your mind and heart for the supper.

ASSUME AN ATTITUDE OF PRAYER AS YOU READ.
WHEN MURRAY PROVIDES A PRAYER, MAKE IT YOUR OWN.

IN REMEMBRANCE OF ME

"Do this in remembrance of me" (Luke 22:19, AM). Is this injunction, really necessary? Can it be possible that I should forget Jesus? Forget Jesus? Jesus, who thought of me in eternity; who forgot His own sorrows on the Cross but never forgets mine; who says to me that a mother will sooner forget her nursing child than He in heaven will forget me. Can I forget Jesus? Jesus, my Sun, my Surety, my Bridegroom; my Jesus, without whose love I cannot live. Can I ever forget Jesus?

Ah, me! how often have I forgotten Jesus. How frequently has my foolish heart grieved Him and prepared all kinds of sorrow for itself by forgetting Jesus. At one time it was in the hour of care, or sin, or grief and at another time it was in prosperity and joy that I allowed myself to be led astray. O my soul, be deeply ashamed that You should ever forget Jesus.

And Jesus will not be forgotten. He will see to it that this will not take place for His own sake. He loves us so dearly that He cannot endure to be forgotten. Our love is to Him His happiness and joy. He requires it from us with a holy strictness. So truly has the eternal Love chosen us that it longs to live in our remembrance every day.

For our sakes He will see to it that He is not forgotten. Jesus always yearns to be with us and beside us. He desires that we taste of His crucified love and the power of His heavenly life. Jesus wills that we should always remember Him.

How I long never more to forget Jesus. Thank God, Jesus will so give Himself to me at the table that He will become to me One never to be forgotten. At the table He will overshadow and satisfy me with His love. He will make His love to me so glorious that my love will always hold Him in remembrance. He will unite Himself with me and give His life in me. Out of the power of His own indwelling Spirit in me, it will not be possible for me to forget Him. I have too much considered it a duty and a work to remember Jesus. Lord Jesus, so fill me with Your joy that it will be impossible for me not to remember You.

Jesus remembers me with a tender love. He desires and will grant that the remembrance of Him will always live in me. For this reason He gives me the new remembrance of His love in the Lord's Supper. I will draw near to His table in this joyful assurance: Jesus will there teach me to remember Him always.

Prayer: My Lord, how wonderful is Your love that you always desire to live in my remembrance—in my love. Lord, You know that my heart cannot be taught to remember You by force. But as Your love dwells in me, thinking of You becomes a joy—no effort or trouble, but the sweetest rest. Lord, my soul praises You for the wonderful grace of the Supper. First, You give Yourself in Your eternal and unchangeable love as the daily food of my soul. O my Lord, at Your table give Yourself to my soul as its food. Be my food every day, and Your love will keep the thought of You ever living in me. Then I will never forget You; no, not for a single moment. For then I will have no life except in Your love. Amen (LT, pp. 74–77).

2. WHAT HAVE YOU LEARNED OR DONE DURING THESE WEEKS OF PREPARATION THAT WILL BEST HELP YOU REMEMBER CHRIST AND HIS LOVE FOR YOU? BRIEFLY DESCRIBE THE TRUTH OR THE EXPERIENCE.

God's visitation the day before FRS

FORGIVENESS

"My blood, which is shed for the forgiveness of sins" (Matt. 26:28, AM). Sin: this word is not to be forgotten at the Lord's table. It is sin that gives us a right to Christ. It is as a Savior from sin that Christ relates to us. It is as sinners that we sit down at the table. If I cannot always come immediately to Christ and appropriate Him, I can always come on the ground of my sin. Sin is the handle by which I can take hold of Christ. I may not be able to lay my hand on Christ and say: Christ is mine. But I can always say: Sin is mine. Then I hear the glad tidings that Christ died for sin. I obtain courage to say: Sin is mine; and Christ, who died for sin, died also for me. Sin: how sweet it is to hear that word from the mouth of Jesus at the table.

And what does my Savior say about sin? He speaks of it only to give the assurance of the forgiveness of sin. That God no more remembers my sin. He no longer counts my sin against me. He does not desire to deal with me in deserved wrath, but He meets me in love as one whose sin is taken away. That is what my Jesus secures for me. He points me to His blood at the table and gives it to me as my own. And that is what you may believe and enjoy, O my soul, when you drink that blood. Ask Him to make known to you the divine glory of this forgiveness as complete, effectual, entire, always valid and eternal. Then you will be able to sing: "Blessed is the man whose transgression is forgiven."

Then will you see how this forgiveness includes in itself all other blessings. For the one of whom God forgives sin, him He also receives, him He loves, him He acknowledges as a child, and gives him the Holy Spirit with all His gifts. The forgiveness of sin is the pledge of entrance into the whole riches of the grace of God. The soul that day by day really enjoys forgiveness in the Lord Jesus will go forth in the joy and power of the Lord.

O what a blessed feast: to know myself to be one with Jesus as a ransomed soul. Blessed it is, because there, while He points with His finger to the sin for which I must be so bitterly ashamed, I can hear this glorious word: "Forgiven." Blessed, because, for the confirmation of this forgiveness and the communication of all its blessing, I am there nourished by the very blood which was shed for forgiveness of sins. Blessed, because in the joy of the forgiveness and the enjoyment of that blood, I am linked again with that Jesus who loves me so wonderfully. Yes, blessed, because I know that in place of sins He now gives me Himself to fill my empty heart, to adorn it with the light and the beauty of His own life. Blessed feast, blessed drinking unto forgiveness of sins!

Prayer: Precious Savior, I am naturally so afraid to look upon my sins, to acknowledge them, and to combat them. In the joy and power of Your forgiveness, I dread this no more. Now I can look upon them as a victor. Help me to love You much, because I have been forgiven much. Amen (LT, pp. 85–88).

DESCRIBE IN YOUR OWN WORDS WHAT YOU FEEL
TOWARD THE LORD JESUS BECAUSE OF HIS FORGIVENESS.
MAKE THIS YOUR PRAYER.

_____

_____

Day 27 ~ Final Preparation for the Lord's Table

"This is My body, which is given for you.
Do this in remembrance of Me."

Luke 22:19

1. BEFORE GOING TO THE LORD'S TABLE TOMORROW, MEDITATE ON WHAT AWAITS YOU THERE. READ, REFLECT, PRAY, AND RESPOND TO THE LORD THROUGH THE FOLLOWING MEDITATIONS BY ANDREW MURRAY. UNDERLINE STATEMENTS THAT ARE ESPECIALLY MEANINGFUL TO YOU SO THAT YOU CAN EASILY REVIEW THEM.

AN EXERCISE OF FAITH

Prayer: Beloved Lord Jesus, You are the desire of my soul. You are He in whom the love of the Father is disclosed to me. You are He who has loved me even unto death on earth. And You still love me in Your glory on high. You are He in whom alone my soul has its life. ... On this holy morning I will prepare myself to go to the table by exercising and confessing anew my faith in You. ...

My Savior, I come to You this morning with the confession that there is nothing in myself on which I can lean. All my experiences confirm to me what You have said of my corruption: that in me, that is, in my flesh, there dwells no good thing. And yet I come to You to lay my claim before You and to take You as mine own. O, my

Lord, my claim rests on the word of my Father that He has given His Son for sinners, that You died for the ungodly. My sinfulness is my claim upon You: You are for sinners. My claim is God's eternal righteousness: You have paid the sin-debt; the guilty must go free. My claim rests on Your love: You have compassion on the wretched. My claim is Your faithfulness: O, my Savior, I have given myself to You and You have received me. What You have begun in me, You will gloriously complete. ... Blessed Lord, unveil Yourself to me, in order that my faith may be truly strong and joyful.

Yes: Lord Jesus, with all Your fullness You are mine. God be praised, I can say this: Your blood is mine: it has atoned for all my sins. Your righteousness is mine: You, Yourself, are my righteousness, and You make me altogether acceptable to the Father. Your love is mine: yes, in all its height and depth and length and breadth is Your love mine. ... All that You have is mine. Your wisdom is mine; Your strength is mine; Your holiness is mine; Your life is mine; Your glory is mine; Your Father is mine. Beloved Lord Jesus, my soul has only one desire this day: that You, my Almighty Friend, would make me with a silent but very powerful activity of faith to behold You, and inwardly appropriate You as my possession. Lord Jesus, in the simplicity of a faith that depends only on You, I say: God be praised, Jesus with all His fullness is mine. ...

Help me now, Lord, to go to Your table in the blessed expectation of new communications out of the treasures of Your love. Let my faith be not only strong, but large: may it cause me to open my mouth wide to receive your holy food.

I stand in need of much today. But what I need above all is this: that I may know my Lord as the daily food of my soul, and that I may comprehend how He will every day be my strength and my life. My desire is that I may understand that not only at the Lord's Supper, but every hour of my life on earth, my Lord Jesus is willing to take the responsibility of my life, to be my life, and to live His life in me.

Beloved Lord, I believe that You have the power to work this in me. I know that Your love is waiting for me, and will take great delight in doing this for me. I believe, Lord, and You will come to help my unbelief. Yes, although I do not thoroughly understand it, I will believe that my Jesus will today communicate Himself anew to me as my life. I will believe that what He does today, He will confirm every day from now on. Yes, my precious Savior, I will this day give myself over to You to dwell in me. And I will believe that You, because You are wholly my possession, will make me ready, come in and take possession of me, and fill me with Yourself. Lord, I do believe; increase this faith within me.

And now, Lord, prepare me and all Your congregation for a blessed observance of the Supper. "Now, unto Him that is able to do exceeding abundantly above all that we ask or think, according to the power that works in us, unto Him be the glory in the Church and in Christ Jesus, unto all generations forever and ever. Amen" (Eph. 3:20-21, AM) (LT, pp. 65–69).

2. REREAD THE STATEMENTS THAT YOU UNDERLINED ABOVE. DRAW A STAR BESIDE THE ONE THAT STANDS OUT AS THE MOST MEANINGFUL.

3. UNDERLINE MEANINGFUL STATEMENTS IN THIS NEXT MEDITATION.

TAKE, EAT

"Take, eat; this is My body which is given for you" (Matt. 26:26; Luke 22:19, AM). When the Lord says this, He points out to us that His body is not so much His as it is ours. He received it and allowed it to be broken on the cross, not for His own sake, but for ours. He now desires that we should look upon it and take it as our own possession. … The fellowship of the Lord's Supper is a fellowship of giving and taking. Blessed giving: blessed taking. – receiving.

Blessed giving: the person gives value to the gift. Who is He that gives? It is my Creator, who comes here to give what my soul needs. It is my Redeemer, who, at the table, will give to me in possession what He has purchased for me.

And what does He give? His body and His blood. He gives the greatest and the best He can bestow. Yes, He gives all that it is possible for Him to give—the broken body which He first offered to the Father as a sacrifice for sin, a sacrifice that filled Him with joy. And what He offered to the Father, to put away sin before Him, He now offers to me, to put away sin in me.

And why does He give this? <u>Because He loves me</u>. He desires to redeem me from death and to bestow on me eternal life in Himself. He gives Himself to me to be the food, the joy, the living power of my soul. O blessed, heavenly giving of eternal love! Jesus gives me His own body: <u>Jesus gives me Himself</u>.

Blessed taking: it is so simple. Just as I receive with my hand the bread that <u>is intended for me</u>, and hold it before me <u>as my own</u>, so by faith in the word, in which Jesus gives Himself to me, I take Him for myself, and I know that He is really mine. The body in which He suffered for sin is my possession: the power of His atonement is mine. The body of Jesus is my food and my life.

I think of my unworthiness, only to find in it my claim on Him, the Righteous One, who died for the unrighteous. I think of my misery only as the poverty and the hunger for which the meal is prepared, this divine bread so lovingly given. <u>What Jesus in His love would give so heartily and willingly, I will as heartily and freely take</u>. ...

Prayer: Blessed God, <u>may my taking conform with Your giving</u>. What You give, I take as a whole. <u>As You give, so I also receive—heartily, undividedly, lovingly</u>. <u>Precious Savior, my taking depends wholly on Your giving</u>.

Come and give Yourself truly and with power in the communion of the Spirit. Come, my eternal Redeemer, and let Your love delight itself and be satisfied in me, while You unfold to me the divine secret of the word: "My body given for you." Yes, Lord, I wait upon You. What You give me as my share in Your broken body, that I will take and eat. And my soul will go from Your Table, joyful and strengthened, to thank You and to serve You. Amen (LT, pp. 70–73).

4. REVIEW "MY PREPARATIONS" LIST ON PAGE 127 AND MAKE FINAL PREPARATIONS FOR THE LORD'S TABLE.

Some people find it meaningful to fast for the time period leading to the Lord's table. You may want to refrain from eating one or more meals, perhaps beginning the evening before the supper, to focus more time in prayer for the service and to heighten your anticipation for the meal.

Day 28 ~ Group Session 4

OPEN WITH PRAYER

Pray that the Lord will complete His work of helping you prepare for the Lord's table. Pray that He will guide each person to live differently because of Christ's love that was perfectly demonstrated on the cross. Give God permission to lead your group to actions they can take together to demonstrate their love and obedience to Him.

SING/LISTEN

Select one or more songs or hymns that focus your attention on Christ and His sacrifice on the cross. Sing them together, read the lyrics, or listen to someone sing them live or from a recording.

REVIEW DAYS 22–27

1. What Scripture, statement, idea, testimony, or illustration that you read this week was most significant or meaningful to you and why?
2. What are some ways you can cultivate your love relationship with God the Father, Son, and Spirit?
3. What are some ways you can demonstrate your love for Christ?
4. What is the connection between love for Christ and obedience to Him?
5. What is Jesus' final command? How is Christ's love compelling you to obey His final command? Is the Lord impressing your group to labor together in obeying His final command? In what ways?
6. What was the battle cry of Moravian missions? (See p. 13.) How is God stirring a similar passion in your mind and heart? Or would you have to confess that you have not yet chosen to love the lost world like that? Pause and pray for a passion to win for Christ the rewards He deserves because He suffered and died.

RESPOND TO THE LORD IN PRAYER

Invite one or more volunteers to lead your group in prayer by responding to what God has been doing and saying in your lives this week and during this session thus far.

Respond to Learning Activities

1. Day 22, activity 4 (p. 96) or day 23, activity 3 (p. 98). Share about your experience of spending time with your Heavenly Father or your walk with your Lord.
2. Day 24, activity 2 (p. 101). What are some ways you sense a desire to demonstrate your love for Christ to a person or group? As your group shares, is there a project the Lord is prompting you to undertake together in ways you cannot accomplish individually?
3. Day 26, activity 1 (p. 106). How would you describe your thoughts and emotions as we approach the time for the Lord's table?
4. Day 26, activity 2 (p. 109). What have you learned or experienced during the past month that will best help you remember Christ and His love for you?
5. Day 26, closing prayer (p. 110). Share your prayer.
6. Day 27 (p. 111). What one statement in Murray's meditations was most meaningful to you and why?

Pray Together

1. In small groups of the same gender provide an opportunity for members to share any personal requests for prayer. Ask one person to pray for each request.
2. Pray that God will prepare and use your pastor and other worship leaders to help your church have a wonderful encounter with the living Christ.
3. Pray that God will guide and complete in all your church family the heart preparations needed so that they can participate in a worthy manner.
4. Close your prayer time in the large group. Spend time in prayers of praise, thanksgiving, and worship expressing to Christ your love and adoration.

Now come to the Lord's table. Worship your wounded Savior. Receive the spiritual food He offers. Remember Him. Rejoice in Him. Look forward to His return and the marriage supper of the Lamb.

PASTOR GUIDE

You are probably reading this section because you realize the importance of preparing your members for the Lord's table (Lord's Supper, Communion, or Eucharist). This resource can help your people focus on Jesus' sacrifice on the cross and help them return to their first love for Christ. Four weeks of daily devotions take your members through a scriptural process that helps them thoroughly examine themselves and get right with God and others before partaking of the holy supper. They will be spiritually prepared to partake in a worthy manner. They will be challenged to live more godly lives of obedience and service to Christ because of His sacrifice for them. I pray that this tool will assist you in helping your people experience genuine renewal of life and vitality for Christ.

If you have not already done so, read the preface before continuing (p. 4). Notice that preparing for and celebrating the Lord's table can be catalysts for renewal and revival. Read the testimony of the Moravian Revival in day 2 (p. 10), when three hundred people fell in love with their wounded Savior at the Lord's table and changed their world.

Since I first published this book, I have heard a variety of testimonies from pastors that have been encouraging.

+ One pastor had an elderly woman with tears in her eyes say, "Pastor, I've never been in love with Jesus like this before."

+ Members of a rural church told their pastor that this was the first time anyone had ever told them what the Lord's Supper was all about. They had previously gone through the ritual without understanding the full meaning.

+ Men told that same pastor that they wanted to get serious about winning others to Christ and asked to go witnessing with him.

+ A First Church pastor said his church had gone through the "worship wars." As members studied reconciliation and forgiveness together, they started calling and visiting others to make their relationships right. Public confessions began that led to much healing in the congregation.

+ Another pastor testified that his members were convicted that they were idolators and began putting away idols of the heart.

+ Homes have been cleansed of moral and spiritual impurities that had been tolerated before.

+ Church leaders who had fought for control of the church repented and surrendered control to Christ, acknowledging His lordship and headship.

I believe the major cause of sickness in the church today is a lack of love for Christ. We have left our first love. Our disobedience, toleration of sin, and acceptance of substitutes for God are symptoms of our departed hearts. We are in a battle for the hearts of God's people. Just as in Elijah's day, God is prepared to turn the hearts of His people back to Himself. The battle is not ours but His. Christ's love for us is the reason we love Him to begin with. Let's lift Him high in the eyes of God's people so that He will draw their hearts back to their first love!

OVERVIEW OF THE FOUR-WEEK SPIRITUAL EMPHASIS

1. **Invitation.** Invite all members to prepare for and attend a sacred assembly of the church around a Lord's table observance. Some churches use deacons to distribute copies of this study to active and inactive church members with an invitation to prepare for this special celebration of the Lord's table.

2. **Personal preparation.** At least four weeks before the date of the Lord's table, distribute copies of *Come to the Lord's Table* to each older youth and adult member. Ask participants to complete the daily devotions and learning activities prior to the weekly small-group sessions.

3. **Small-group sessions.** Use ongoing classes, small groups, cell groups, or home meetings for church members to meet and process what they have studied during the week. Days 7, 14, 21, and 28 provide guidance for a meaningful group experience as members help one another prepare to meet at the Lord's table. Members will need to complete days 1–6 before the first session.

4. **Sermon series.** Select sermon topics and plan worship experiences that complement the preparation members are making in their personal study and group sessions. Focus on the meaning and purposes of the Lord's table (remembering Christ's sacrifice on the cross and looking ahead to the marriage supper of the Lamb), the importance and process of personal preparation, the value and way of restoring relationships in the body of Christ, and the appropriate responses of a people returning to Christ as their first love.

5. **Pre-Communion service.** Conduct a pre-Communion service (described on p. 120) as a time of final preparation for individual members and your church body as a whole.

6. **The Lord's table.** Spend your entire service focusing on the holy supper and Jesus' sacrifice on the cross, which the supper represents. Build your message and worship on the themes of the supper and the cross.

7. **Love feast (optional).** Sometime following the Lord's table, conduct a love feast (described on p. 123) to feast, worship, and share testimonies of God's work in your lives. Celebrate His bountiful love.

USING COME TO THE LORD'S TABLE

1. **Pray.** Your church belongs to the Lord Jesus, who is its Head. Begin this process with prayer. Ask the Lord to guide you to Himself. Invite prayer warriors and prayer-ministry teams to bathe this season in prayer. Pray specifically for every church member. Pray that this will be a time of renewal and revival for every life and family. Pray that lost people will be converted during this season.

2. **Decide on the season for the emphasis.** You can use this guide any time of the year. The season leading up to Easter may be an especially meaningful time because it coincides with the last supper Jesus celebrated with His disciples before going to the cross. Some churches may schedule a special Maundy Thursday service during Easter week to commemorate the last supper. Others may choose to use the study in the winter leading up to a special Christmas observance of the Lord's table, with a love feast on New Year's Eve. Others choose a time around Thanksgiving. Sometimes now is the most appropriate time. Use this resource to prepare for your next scheduled Lord's table. You can also use it as spiritual preparation for revival or evangelistic meetings.

3. **Determine the schedule.** Read this section of suggestions and decide whether you will conduct a pre-Communion service and a love feast in conjunction with the Lord's table observance. Set the dates on your church calendar.

If possible, clear the four weeks for this emphasis of competing events or church activities so that people will not be distracted from their preparations.

4. **Order books.** Write to LifeWay Resources Customer Service; One LifeWay Plaza; Nashville, TN 37234; phone toll free 800-458-2772; order online at LifeWay.com; fax 615-251-5933; email orderentry@lifeway.com; or visit the LifeWay Christian Store serving you. Each participant needs a personal copy in order to benefit from the personal-application questions throughout the study. Remember to allow time not only for shipping but also for members to complete the first six daily devotions prior to their first small-group session.

5. **Invite members.** In the Old Testament sacred assemblies, especially the emergency ones that often led to revival, everyone was expected to attend. Because the Lord's table was instituted for the body of Christ, make a special effort to get every adult, youth, and older child to participate in both preparation and attendance. This study holds great potential as an opportunity for renewal or revival among your members. I suggest that you send a personal letter to each member or family and strongly encourage their participation and attendance. Encourage participation from the pulpit and through regular church-information channels. You might even use a phone

campaign to ensure that every member knows the value and seriousness of this time of sacred assembly. Prepare a special sermon to extend the initial invitation to a sacred assembly.

6. **Distribute books.** Distribute books to members at least a week prior to the first small-group session.

7. **Plan services.** Coordinate plans for the services with the leaders of music, drama, media, and other ministries. Make a special effort to make the worship experiences especially meaningful and memorable. Encourage planners to be creative in designing the atmosphere and services.

8. **Future use of *Come to the Lord's Table.*** After using this book for the first time, you may want to encourage members to review it before future celebrations of the Lord's table. Your church may want to plan an annual review of *Come to the Lord's Table* in years to come and encourage newcomers to complete the study in preparation for the sacred assembly at the Lord's table. Form groups for newcomers and even for those who are reviewing.

A PRE-COMMUNION SERVICE

A pre-Communion service provides a time for members to gather and help one another make final preparation for the Lord's table. Though much will take place in small groups, a church may need a corporate time for reconciliation, prayer, and worship in preparation for the Lord's table.

At the service members can pray for one another, reconcile broken relationships, confess and seek forgiveness for publicly known sin, and recommit their lives to Christ's lordship. Although you could celebrate the Lord's table without having a pre-Communion service, I highly recommend that you seriously consider providing time for members to prepare together.

The Bible does not prescribe what must be done to fully prepare for the Lord's table. This study provides guidance for personal preparation. Small groups will provide opportunities for members to deal with issues for which they need prayer and help in the confidentiality of smaller, same-gender groups. But your church as a whole could benefit by setting aside a time before the Lord's table to make final preparation together. Below are suggested components of a pre-Communion service, but you have great latitude in designing this service. Ask the Lord to guide you in customizing a service for your church, including elements you sense would meet the needs of your members. If this is new to you, walk by faith, trusting the Lord to guide you. If you need help, invite a fellow pastor or a denominational leader to assist you this first time.

1. **Who should come?** In the Old Testament all who could understand were invited to sacred assemblies. Older children, youth, and adults should certainly be included. Even younger children can benefit by seeing adults take seriously their faith and their relationships with

Christ and His church. Ask members to come for an open-ended period of time. You may want to hire child-care workers for babies and preschoolers so that every adult member can participate in the service.

2. **Fasting before supper.** Some members may want to fast before the Lord's table. Invite those who choose to fast to begin by skipping the meal just prior to the pre-Communion service and continuing their fast until the Lord's table. This should not be legalistic, public, or mandatory. Allow personal freedom here.

3. **Service elements.** Choose from the following elements to design your service or plan your own activities as God guides you.

   + **Music and singing.** Sing hymns or provide special music related to the cross, the atonement, the Lord's Supper, forgiveness, Christ's love, and similar topics.

   + **Scripture reading.** Read Scriptures related to the same topics. Include others that call members to deal seriously with specific sins. Also consider responsive or choral readings of Scripture.

   + **Message.** If you preach, use a brief message on the importance of preparing to partake of the Lord's table in a worthy manner. Invite members to finalize their preparations for the supper. Keep in mind that the focus of this service is on responding to the Lord, not just teaching and learning.

Use the message to call for members to respond. Reserve most of your time for responses.

+ **Testimonies.** Invite testimonies about ways God has worked in members' lives during their preparation for the Lord's table, including experiences of God's love and grace, spiritual breakthroughs, victories over besetting sin, reconciled relationships, confessions of newfound faith in Christ, and so forth. As the pastor, you may hear testimonies from members prior to the service. Ask small-group leaders to identify persons who might have meaningful testimonies. Enlist some to share. You may want to videotape testimonies so that you can control the focus and time allotted to each.

+ **Prayer.** Provide for a variety of prayer experiences.

   –Provide soft music for a time of silent prayer and meditation.

   –Someone could sing or play a recorded version of "The Altar" by Ray Boltz and Steve Millikan and open the altar for individuals, couples, or families to kneel and pray.

   –Break into smaller groups of four to eight, preferably with members of the same gender. Invite group members to ask one another the question, How may we pray for you? Then have one or two in the group pray for each request. Requests might include—

❑ besetting sin they can't defeat;

❑ a broken relationship that needs mending (unforgiveness, bitterness, the need to make restitution, etc.);

❑ a wounded spirit because of the past that keeps them at a distance from the Heavenly Father;

❑ materialism or love for the world;

❑ unbelief;

❑ wrong motives;

❑ prayerlessness;

❑ apathy;

❑ disobedience;

❑ moral failure;

❑ pride;

❑ busyness.

–Provide an opportunity for members to come and share a need or confess a sin and pray with a pastor, a minister, an elder, a deacon, or a prayer warrior. If appropriate and only with permission, share some of these needs with the congregation and invite other members to surround the person during the prayer.

+ **Public confession.** The general guideline for the public confession of sin is to confess the sin as broadly as the offense. Reserve public confession for sin that has become publicly known or was committed against the church or many of its members. I recommend that the pastor or another spiritual leader personally screen each person's desire for public confession to make sure it is appropriate. Those receiving people for prayer should agree on a procedure to follow about public confession. Following a confession, guide the congregation to express its forgiveness, invite the person to pray aloud and ask God for forgiveness, invite members to gather around him or her to pray for mercy and victory, or in some other way respond to the request for forgiveness.

+ **Reconciliation.** Encourage members to go to one another to ask forgiveness or to be reconciled over offenses God has identified. Provide soft music. Ask those who don't sense a need to reconcile to pray for their fellow church members who need to forgive and be reconciled. Don't rush this time. You may want to share guidelines similar to these:

–If you are the offender, acknowledge your sin and say, "Please forgive me." Don't give excuses or try to justify your actions. Don't imply or make accusations about wrong on the other person's part. That is their responsibility.

–If you sense that a broken relationship exists and don't know what is wrong, say, "I sense there may be a broken relationship between us, but I'm not sure I know why. Help me understand what I need to do to be reconciled with you."

–If you miss getting to reconcile with anyone, contact him or her after the service.

- **Invitation to receive Christ.** Often in history, people were converted during the season of preparation for the Lord's table. I was in a church in Florida where a Satan worshiper came to faith in Christ during a pre-Communion service. You may want to extend an invitation to anyone who wants to confess faith in Christ.
- **Invitation to follow Christ in baptism.** As people are confronted with the need to obey Christ in their personal preparations, some may come to the conviction that they need to obey Christ in baptism, having already professed faith in Christ. I was in upstate New York when a woman came forward with just such a decision. The leaders arranged for a baptismal service the next morning before the Lord's Supper. What rejoicing follows decisions like this.
- **Open-ended closing.** As you close the service, invite members to continue responding to the Lord as long as needed. They may want to remain for prayer, continue seeking to reconcile relationships, or pray with a leader.

A LOVE FEAST (AGAPE MEAL)

The New Testament indicates that the churches had a mealtime they called a love feast or *agape* (Greek word for *love*) meal. We don't know exactly what took place at these meals, but they were more than an observance of the Lord's Supper. Some groups in history have experienced wonderful Christian fellowship and love at times they called a love feast.

This optional activity would add to your experience of the Lord's table. Consider gathering for a love feast sometime following the Lord's table. It could be the same day or the following week. Consider the following ideas and suggestions in planning your meal.

1. **Meal.** The meal can be simple or complex. Moravians serve a sweet bun and a cup of coffee for their love feasts. You could have a more extensive meal, a potluck meal, or a full-blown dinner on the grounds. One key to keep in mind is that the fellowship is to be the emphasis, not the food. Don't just eat and leave.

2. **Singing.** The service should be light and more spontaneous than structured. Consider conducting a hymn sing featuring requests, favorites, or songs that focus on love for Christ and on unity and Christian love for one another.

3. **Testimonies.** Invite testimonies on what God has done during the four-week focus on the Lord's table. Start by asking members to share testimonies around their tables or in small groups of about eight. These should be voluntary, so don't go around the circle. Testimonies could include victories over sin, lives changed, relationships reconciled, deeper experiences of Christ's love, experiences from a date or an outing with the Heavenly

Father, experiences during the walk with Jesus, insights into Christ's sacrifice, feelings and memories of the Lord's table service itself, and so forth. After members have shared in small groups, call for testimonies to be shared with the large group.

4. **Affirmations.** Too often we fail to say thank you or to affirm what God is doing in and through those around us. Provide an opportunity for public thank-you's or for affirming blessings in the lives of others. Invite people to finish this sentence: "I thank God for [name] because. ..." You might even recognize some groups of people for a group thank-you, such as teachers, workers with preschoolers, ushers, or others who may seldom receive thanks for their ministry to the body. Think of other ways for members to express love and appreciation for members of the body of Christ.

5. **Love offering.** If you decide to have a love offering, announce the opportunity early in the study or at least by the time of the Lord's table so that people will have time to reflect, pray, and prepare. Invite members to consider giving a special love offering above their regular giving to express an extra thank-You to Christ for His sacrifice. Decide in advance how you will use this special offering. You might use it for church members' benevolent needs, as the church in Acts did with gifts like that of Barnabas in Acts 4:32-37. You might use it for a special mission project. You might give it to a church on the mission field or to a needy church in your own city. If you are willing to manage the process, the offerings could be more than money. People might choose to give other things of value for use by others in the body of Christ or things that could be sold, such as jewelry, used cars, stocks, volunteer service for a particular project, and so on. You might even suggest that people who have identified idols of the heart they need to give away (rather than destroyed because of their wickedness) might bring those as their offerings. This offering could include a boat, a collection, toys, material things that have captured their love, and so forth. Let this be a matter of joy, not obligation. Encourage people to have fun deciding what to give and to have joy in blessing others as they use the gifts to show God's love to one another.

6. **Prayers.** Invite volunteers to stand and pray prayers of thanksgiving, praise, adoration, and love to Christ for His love and for the blessings of the past few weeks.

SMALL-GROUP LEADER GUIDE

Select leaders for small groups who will serve as spiritual facilitators of the group process. These may be leaders of existing classes, small groups, or cell groups. Or you may enlist and orient leaders especially for this study of *Come to the Lord's Table*.

Come to the Lord's Table is designed for four small-group sessions. Read the preceding pastor guide to understand the entire process. Plan for 60- to 90-minute sessions. If you see that people need more help than this time allows, you may want to plan for longer sessions or be available after the sessions to help.

The session plans are built into the daily devotions. Days 7, 14, 21, and 28 recommend activities for prayer, singing, reviewing content, sharing responses to learning activities, and preparing for the Lord's table. Review the plans and select questions and activities that you sense will be most meaningful, appropriate, or helpful. You may want to enlist an assistant or a coleader so that you can discuss the group's needs week by week and help one another determine the best process for your group.

In addition to the session plans on the days mentioned, the following suggestions may also be helpful.

GROUP SESSION 1 (DAY 7)

If your group members are not well acquainted, begin your first session by inviting members to introduce themselves. Ask them to share information about their immediate families, something about their spiritual pilgrimages, and/or how they started attending this church.

Briefly overview the process your church is undertaking over the next month. Encourage members to prepare spiritually by completing the daily devotions. Ask them to commit to a vow of confidentiality. We want to help one another, not hurt one another.

At the end of the session, preview the coming week. Instruct members to read days 8–13 before the next group session. Read the titles of those days. Encourage members to begin this time of personal examination with seriousness and a willingness to experience the Lord's refining process so that they will be worthy guests at His table.

Mention the activities in day 13 (p. 60) that suggest family participation. Ask members to preview them early in the week so that they can schedule a time for their families to complete the activities before the next group session.

GROUP SESSION 2 (DAY 14)

This session will require more time for prayer for one another. As you plan, allow at least 30 minutes for the small-group prayer activity described at the end of the session (p. 65). If you don't get through with "Review Days 8–13" and "Respond to Learning Activities," move to prayer anyway. If time remains after prayer, you can go back and finish your sharing on the other topics.

I've encouraged you to divide your group into smaller groups of three to five persons of the same gender. This smaller grouping allows increased opportunities for personal sharing and ministry to one another. It also provides a less threatening group if a person needs to share needs or make confidential prayer requests. Emphasize that information shared in small-group times should be kept confidential. Ask members not to cause offenses by gossiping outside the small group.

The same-gender recommendation is very important. Some sin issues that may surface do not need to be shared in a mixed group (and often would not be shared in a mixed group). Group men with men and women with women. If space permits, you may want to encourage small groups to spread out so that they can talk without fear of being overheard by others.

To preview the coming week, instruct members to read days 15–20 before the next group session. Read the titles of those days. Explain that the lessons on reconciliation and forgiveness may be difficult if members have many broken relationships. Day 17 (p. 74) has been designed to provide time to restore right relationships. Encourage members to do the hard work for the sake of joy and freedom that wait on the other side of reconciliation.

GROUP SESSION 3 (DAY 21)

To preview the coming week, instruct members to read days 22–27 before the next group session. Read the titles of those days. Day 23 (p. 97) encourages members to take a walk and spend half an hour or more talking to the Lord in prayer. Suggest that members feel free to adjust their schedule of lessons to fit this walk into the week. Encourage them to make a special effort to complete these lessons, even if they need extra days following the Lord's table to complete them all.

GROUP SESSION 4 (DAY 28)

Preferably, you will conduct this session prior to the observance of the Lord's table. This will provide one final time of preparation for partaking in a worthy manner. Be sure to review dates and times for all of the events related to the Lord's table.